Wakefield Press

I0203799

Slow Boat to Mongolia

Lydia Laube resists jet planes and tourist destinations, firmly believing that 'the journey is the thing, not the destination'. Seen often in China clutching a ticket and hopping on a train hoping it was the right one, Lydia's single-minded determination and enthusiasm invariably carries her through. A nurse by profession, Lydia has delivered babies and tended clinics all over the world. And growing up on a farm in the mid-north of South Australia made her no stranger to mutton, a distinct advantage to a traveller visiting Outer Mongolia.

Slow Boat to Mongolia is Lydia Laube's third book. Her first two, *Behind the Veil: An Australian nurse in Saudi Arabia* and *The Long Way Home*, have been Australian best-sellers.

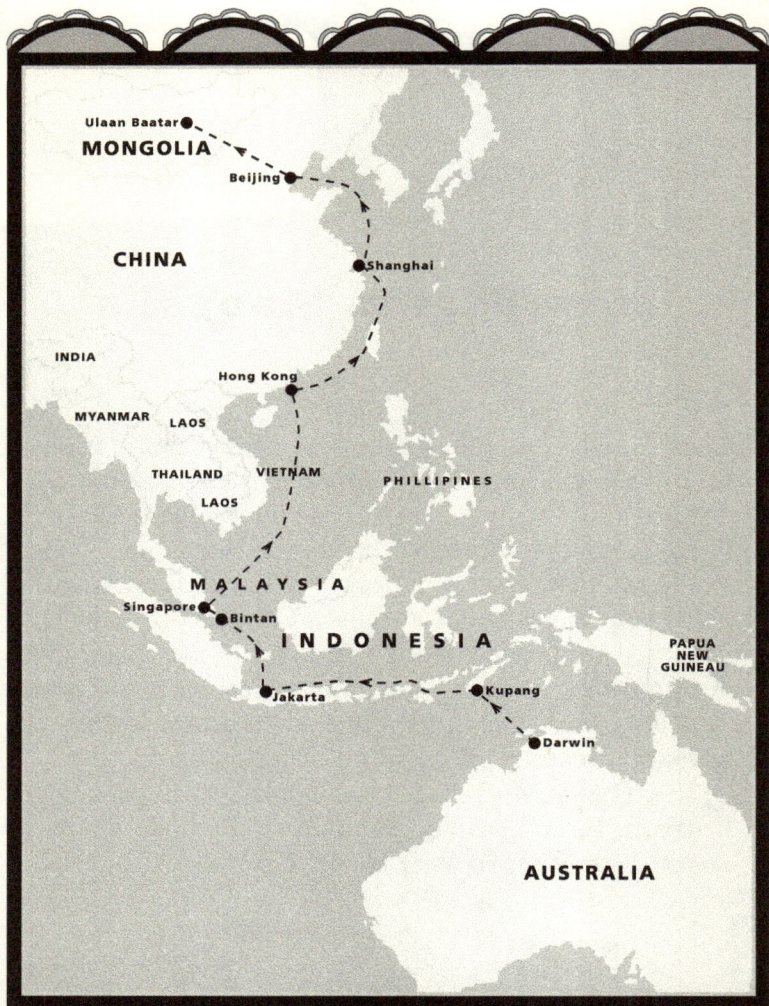

Slow Boat to Mongolia

LYDIA LAUBE

Wakefield
Press

Wakefield Press
16 Rose Street
Mile End
South Australia 5031
www.wakefieldpress.com.au

First published 1997
Reprinted 2020

Designed by Nick Stewart, design BITE, Adelaide
Typeset by Clinton Ellicott, Adelaide

National Library of Australia Cataloguing-in-Publication entry

Laube, Lydia, 1948–   .
Slow boat to Mongolia.

ISBN 978 1 86254 418 5.

1. Laube, Lydia, 1948–   – Journeys. 2. Mongolia – Description
and travel. 3. China – Description and travel. I. Title.

915.17304

Contents

1 Kupang or bust

The Sunday evening crowd relaxed at the water's edge of the Darwin Yacht Club. A full tropical moon, fiery red, rose up out of the sea and turned to gold as we talked idly of places and people. Somebody was talking about Outer Mongolia. My attention was riveted. Outer Mongolia! What a mystical pull those two small words had.

'I'd like to go there,' I said.

'Nobody goes there.' The voice sounded gloomy, detached.

Why didn't anybody go there? How tantalising. It was as if my fate were sealed in that moment. I knew at once that I could not resist. Go there I would and just as soon as I could arrange it. I could make my long-planned visit to China, a place I had wanted to see since the days when it had been closed to travellers, and try to reach Outer Mongolia from there. Once, when I had been working in Hong Kong, I had travelled to the border so that I could say that in some small way I had seen China. It had been just a tempting few steps away but, later that day, in the same place, five Hong Kong policemen had been killed in a fracas with their communist neighbours. I did not go back.

Despite starting with only vague ideas about Outer Mongolia – a remote exotic place, at the end of the earth, where dashing wild men galloped their brilliant horses across limitless steppes – I soon put my hands on everything that had ever been written about it. Few westerners had visited this little explored place and to go there would make me a pioneer, one of the first.

Outer Mongolia's communist portals had only recently been opened, just a crack, to allow selected tourists through. The major obstacle was a visa, a favour the Mongolian authorities confer with great reluctance on decadent capitalists travelling independently. Visas were only issued on an invitation from a Mongolian, and not knowing a lot of Mongolians prepared to invite me, all my enquiries in Australia came to a dead end. Then I heard that the elusive visa might be obtained in Hong Kong or Beijing. That would do me.

I also read that Mongolia was a traveller, not a tourist, destination, and only for hardy, adventurous people who were not averse to a diet that was almost exclusively mutton. This posed no threat to me. I had been raised on it.

Out came the map. I would travel in my preferred manner: by sea and land. It looked easy: I could take a short sail over the Timor Sea to Kupang in Timor, hop from island to island up the Indonesian archipelago to Singapore by inter-island boat, find a vessel plying between Singapore and Hong Kong that would have me on board, take the ship that sails regularly from Hong Kong to Shanghai, and then travel by train, on the Trans Siberian Express, as far as Ulaan Baatar, the capital of Outer Mongolia. It sounded simple.

My research into sailing from Australia revealed that

the only hope of a commercial passage out of Darwin was to Bali or islands west on one of the occasional cruise ships. Such an exercise requires about two hundred dollars a day and dressing for dinner every night. Other highlights are afternoons spent in the hairdressing salon and being taken ashore at ports of call to view the locals, who are flashed past the air-conditioned bus provided for the inspection tour like exhibits at a sideshow. Mentally flipping through my travel wardrobe of three shirts and two pairs of pants, I decided it was not for me. I would suit Indonesia's Pelni ships better. All I had to do was to get to Kupang to connect with one.

There is a twice-weekly plane from Darwin to Kupang, but the airline concerned was not one I would fly with by choice. During the dry season in Darwin it is not difficult to find passage or work on yachts, many of which are heading north to Asian ports. I advertised on notice boards where the boats moor and got many offers, probably thanks to the joker who altered my ad from, 'Female requires passage to Kupang – working or paying,' to 'Female requires passage to Kupang – working or playing'! They are an uncouth lot in the Territory, which is probably why I like them. I was offered legitimate rides to Africa, the Cocos Islands and Perth, and the gypsy in my soul found it difficult to refuse. But Outer Mongolia was my goal.

Not long afterwards I was enjoying another Sunday evening at the yacht club. Dusk was settling over the tide coming in across the sand flats as I sat down at one of the wooden tables on the edge of the small cliff overlooking the beach. A man at the other end of the table was gazing out to sea. After a while he turned around.

'Not bad is it?' I said.

'Blood oath.' This enthusiastic reply came from Doug, a smallish man, not young but deeply tanned and from what I could tell, very fit. He told me he had sailed to Darwin from Papua New Guinea to compete in the world-famous Darwin to Ambon boat race.

Having watched the start of the race the day before, I felt qualified to pass judgment on his plans.

'I hate to be the bearer of bad news, but the race left yesterday.'

'I know,' he groaned, 'I missed it.'

Now I was intrigued. 'How do you miss the beginning of a race you want to compete in?'

'My crew were in gaol for getting in a brawl in a pub. My female crew! Nice Irish and Norwegian girls.'

But this was not his only problem. This jolly sixty-year-old was a walking illustration of Murphy's law. On his way around Cape York to Darwin he had run into a storm which had washed huge waves over his yacht. He had broken three ribs trying to stay afloat and his dingy and outboard motor were washed overboard. A valiant but stupid crew member had jumped in after them and only with much difficulty had been pulled back on board. The dingy was still out on the heaving seas doing an imitation of the *Marie Celeste*.

After the brawl, Doug had needed to pay the two thousand five hundred dollars necessary to bail his crew out of gaol because, as the ship's captain, he was held responsible for their behaviour. He had then sacked them all.

We spent a great evening chatting, and I told Doug about my plans and my search for a passage to Kupang. The next Sunday he was at the club again. He greeted me with the welcome news that he had arranged to take a charter load of tourists to Kupang in a month and that if I wished I could come along. I was delighted.

I went to inspect his boat. She was twenty-five metres long, and neat and trim, and she certainly looked safe enough for me. What I hadn't reckoned on was the safety of the skipper.

Doug's calamities continued. He invited a crowd of us out for a day of fishing and an overnight party, but the engine broke down and we could not go. He advertised a sunset cruise to make some funds to cover his losses and got eighty replies. But the engine played up again that afternoon, and that jaunt fizzled out too. His boat was chartered to take a mob of seventeen tourists around the coast to the Kimberleys. In preparation Doug bought a new dingy and an outboard motor – then dropped the two thousand dollar motor into the drink while loading it onto the ship. When he went ashore to buy another, a fire broke out in the engine room. The automatic fire extinguishers were activated and the foam made a terrible mess. The fire did more than six thousand dollars worth of damage to the engine and boat. And to cap it all he lost three and a half thousand dollars from the fares to the Kimberleys. It didn't augur well.

But wait. There's more! Days before our estimated departure for Kupang, when all was fixed and ready to go and I had bought a ticket on the Pelni line's *Dobronsolo*, which calls at Kupang *en route* to Jakarta every fortnight, Doug was arrested! And so was his boat. It was impounded.

When Doug had bought the yacht the previous year, the former owner had failed to mention that it was heavily mortgaged. Law authorities had been searching for Doug for months. Warrants were out for him all over Australia and Melanesia. Of course he was innocent, but that did not help the boat out of its watery gaol and over to Kupang in time to meet the *Dobronsolo*.

2 From bemos to boats

At the same time as the dramas with Doug were going on, Australia fell out with Indonesia. Timor was preparing for the twentieth anniversary of its invasion by Indonesia, and trouble was expected. Angry mobs of Indonesians, protesting against our support for the Fretilin movement, assailed the Australian consulate in Jakarta and burned our flag in the street. Visas for East Timor's capital, Dili, or for overland travel within the country, were cancelled.

There was now no other way to get to Kupang except on an airline I had always said I would never use. When I told my friends my fate they sang me what they claimed was Merpati's theme song: 'It's Merpati, and I'll die if I want to' to the tune of 'It's my party, and I'll cry if I want to'.

But it was my only chance to get to Kupang and with some trepidation I boarded the plane.

The first thing I noticed was that many of the plane's signs were written in German, remnants from its previous owner. This consoled me to some extent but I couldn't help a passing thought about why they had sold it. Had it been faulty, worn, resurrected from some accident . . .

The hostesses, however, were neat and smiling in their sky-blue uniforms, and we even got a decent meal. Real food, in a plastic box, that looked safe and edible. I have been on small Indonesian airlines before, and the food is usually neither. After a smooth one-hour flight, about five hundred kilometres across the Timor Sea, we had the novelty of arriving in Kupang, an authorised port of entry into Indonesia, at the same time that we had left Darwin.

The immigration officer gave me the usual sixty-day on-the-spot tourist visa for Australians and then I approached Customs nervously, having heard horror stories of the treatment of other travellers. They were a very severe looking lot and obviously people not to be trifled with, but I should have put my prejudices on hold. It was a breeze, if a bit embarrassing as the bemused customs men examined the contents of my grossly over-weight luggage full of jar after jar of face cream, vitamin pills and food. I had very little in the bodily apparel line. My equipage this trip consisted of one smallish wheelable case (swapped for The Monster of previous voyages, which had inconveniently required a strong man in attendance), a big overnight bag, also with wheels, my trusty ton-weight handbag, which should be licensed as a lethal weapon, and the essential umbrella. Travelling light again.

Flushed with my success at having run the gauntlet of immigration and customs unscathed, I met the representative from the Flobamor, Kupang's poshest hotel. He told me that the hotel was the local agent for Pelni and that my ticket was ready in their office. I was happy to take advantage of the ride he offered into town in the hotel's mini bus.

My first impression of West Timor was of a sparsely populated, dry and rocky place, but the weather was pleasantly warm. The country has the same climate as Darwin and this was the dry season. The Portuguese established a settlement in West Timor in the middle of the seventeenth century. Later the Dutch arrived and gradually elbowed their way in so that, by the middle of the eighteenth century, the Portuguese had retreated to the eastern end of the island. When independence was won from Holland in 1945, the Dutch half became part of the new Indonesian republic, but the other half remained Portuguese.

In 1974 Portugal discarded its colonies and East Timor declared itself independent under the control of the Fretilin Party. Indonesia would have none of this freedom in their midst, however, and in December 1975 launched a brutal full-scale invasion of East Timor. Members of the Fretilin movement fought a courageous three-year guerilla war, but starvation and disease, caused by a lack of medicine and food, affected most of the country and almost extinguished the army. Almost – Fretilin is still active. Every now and then there is a blaze of patriotism from a small group hidden in the remote hills.

The desire for freedom dies hard.

Timor was closed to travellers for many years following the invasion but in 1989 Indonesia, feeling that the country was sufficiently suppressed, opened it again. In 1991, however, participants in a Timorese protest at the Dili cemetery were massacred by Indonesian troops. Since then crossing the border overland has been forbidden.

I found no sign of any problems in Kupang. There may have been difficulties in Dili, but I wasn't allowed to go there. I had visited Portuguese Timor years ago. It had been a lovely unspoiled place. I had stayed in Dili and

Baukau, a delightful cool retreat in the mountains, and I had crossed the island by market truck in the company of large numbers of raucous chooks and pigs. There had been no bus in those days and few travellers. I did not particularly regret not being able to return.

On the hotel bus I met two Australian men who had come to collect their yacht after competing in the Darwin–Ambon race. This time I was offered a guaranteed passage on a boat between Kupang and Darwin, but it was going the wrong way! These gents told me that Timorese ports were closed to foreign yachts, except to race entrants, because of the trouble anticipated with the twentieth anniversary remembrance protests. Indonesia was also celebrating its fiftieth anniversary of independence from Dutch rule, which the Timorese may have felt was rubbing salt in their wounds.

I was warned not to discuss politics.

The Hotel Flobamor, having got me in its clutches, made a determined effort to retain me for the three days I had to wait until the *Dobronsolo* came, *if* she was on time. I was able to negotiate a reasonable price for a room with far more facilities than I needed and when I left, was amused to receive a bill headed, '*Stremline Gues Accoun*'.

The hotel was built around courtyards in the Dutch style and, although old, was comfortable. Its main disadvantage was that it was several kilometres from the main part of town on the airport highway (or to be more accurate, high-track; they don't go for roads much in Timor).

I knew I was back in Asia when the first room I was shown had no light. Nor did it appear to have had one for a long time, judging by the state of the fixture on the wall, which presumably had been constructed to contain the light.

This did not deter the staff from trying to rent the room. I may be a simple soul with few needs and wants, but one of them is a perverse and determined desire to have proper lights to find my way about by night.

I pointed this out to the porter, and we set off again, lumping my belongings downstairs in search of another room. There was no lift. The next room had two lights, both worked, but one gave me the obligatory electric shock, so thereafter I left it alone. I had not forgotten the need to approach all electrical devices in Asia with caution.

There were the other usual niceties: switches hanging off walls, and bare wires on appliances. As I left the room the next morning, I turned off the air-conditioner, which promptly shot out a great sheet of green flame and blew up with a loud bang. This was all very entertaining, but being aware that it was not provided to amuse me, I reported it to the front desk, thinking that it would be the last I would see of air-conditioning for my visit. To my great surprise it had been fixed when I returned later that day.

Looking over the top of the courtyard wall at the back of the *Flobamor* I could see life in Timor. There, in direct contrast to the smart facade of the hotel, I saw squat thatched humpies – squalid native huts with tiny cobbled alleys between them. Pigs, chooks and naked children ran around in a world very different from that enjoyed by guests in the hotel.

Next morning a convention of roosters loudly announced daylight under my window and this summons got me to breakfast early. This commodity was served al fresco in a dining area flanked by attractive gardens and was, I was proudly informed, 'All same Beaufort.' The Beaufort, being an elegant hotel in Darwin, would be thrilled to know this.

I had some anaemic toast, which had only been briefly introduced to the toaster, with Vegemite (no prizes for guessing who their most frequent western visitors are, and eggs 'face up', fried in coconut oil on a gas burner on site.

I shared my table with an American couple who were travelling around the islands in their yacht. It sounds a fabulous journey to make but, given the option, I would have chosen the Pelni cattle boat. The American man was thoroughly obnoxious, telling the cook in whingeing tones that he hadn't fried his egg properly and pushing him aside to do it himself. I don't care how someone cooks my eggs as long as I don't have to do it.

After breakfast I decided to go to town in a bemo, the local public transport system. Bemos are tiny Colt vans that people fill until they are packed to the gunwales. They are painted in brilliant colours and patterns and given exotic and varied names. I went out, rightly so, in *Exodus* and came back again in *Jesus*.

The bemos were lit up like Christmas trees, complete with flashing lights, decorations and garlands. Their destinations were identified by the number of lamps on the roof – one, two or three lamps for different stops. The drivers always played incredibly loud music through multiple loudspeakers attached to stereos that were always turned full on. The locals' ears must be immune to the deafening blast that hits you in the face as you climb aboard. But it was the obscene songs they played that gave me a bigger jolt. I felt quite assaulted when I clambered into a bemo for the first time to be greeted by the deafening sounds of a voice screaming in English, 'She's a bitch.' The words soon changed into great blasts of sexually explicit lyrics with liberal use of four-letter words. I stared thunderstruck at the other passengers, who showed no sign that they understood, or were in the slightest way offended. Later I encountered it so often that I almost became immune to it.

I soon also learned to cling to the bemo's overhead

rail, otherwise, wedged as I usually was into a space only big enough for a pygmy with one buttock, I would fly off the seat at the first corner and land in another person's lap. No one else did this. I guess they were conditioned to bemo travel and had acquired the art of balancing on them like sailors do on a ship.

Despite these drawbacks, bemos were very cheap and a great way to get around. I could zip all over town and even out into the countryside for twenty cents. I went to a lot of places I didn't mean to go to, but I had a good look at the town and met crowds of people. Everyone seemed friendly, although more reserved than people on other Indonesian islands I have been to. When I entered a bemo, scaling the back-door step and squeezing in to land on someone's knees, more likely than not I would greet them by saying, '*Salamat pagi*' (Good morning) and they would reply courteously but without the usual beaming smiles I was accustomed to in places like Bali. The West Timorese are not as used to foreigners as the Balinese, and they probably found it odd for someone to be travelling alone, especially a woman. But once, when I was hopelessly lost, and had travelled a long way out of town, the bemo driver finally turned to me and asked, '*Dimana?*' (Where are you going?).

'The museum,' I said.

No, no, that was not where I was going at all. He stopped the bemo and all the passengers looked at me.

I laughed and said, '*Tida apa apa*', an Indonesian version of 'She'll be right.'

At once the passengers joined forces and began to laugh and talk to me, advising me where to go and when to get off. The driver meanwhile got out and flagged down another bemo going in the opposite direction, told the driver where to take me and put me aboard, refusing my proffered payment.

This happened several times afterwards, and I found that as soon as people realised that I was interested in them and their culture, especially when I would attempt to use what I knew of their language, great smiles would illuminate their formerly serious faces.

I was surprised by Kupang (its population over 400,000), the capital of East Nusatenggara Province and the largest town in West Timor. I had thought it would be a large village but, although it retains this ambience, there were many big new buildings and it was spread out over several kilometres.

I was told, however, that the main tourist enticement was the front of the cement factory, which had become a site of pilgrimage for photographers with a perverted sense of humour wishing to record for posterity the sign – in letters two metres high – that proclaims it to be the 'Semen Factory'. Despite this distraction, Kupang is well off the main tourist trails, although Captain Bligh did make an unplanned stay there when he too was having problems with a pugnacious crew.

Downtown Kupang was strikingly clean, but the footpaths were death traps consisting of uneven bricks and open drains so deep that to fall in would require a ladder to get out. There were very few tourists to be seen, which was a blessing, as the locals did not, as so often elsewhere in Asia, pursue me with tatty cultural artefacts for sale but left me well alone. I found no tourist trash or even postcards in the shops. But for all of Kupang's tourist innocence, the iniquitous karaoke had found its way in and was aptly called 'bom bom'!

I bought fruit from sellers on the footpaths – bananas and wonderful mandarins that were green outside and looked unripe but inside were exquisite. And no one hassled me or tried to cheat me. There was just the occasional, 'Hello Missis.'

Avoiding the one tourist trap restaurant, I ate at *rumah makans*, small roadside eating houses that had good cheap food. There were several on the cliffs above the shore where you could eat while looking out across the bay at the cornflower blue water and sky and the ships riding at anchor or passing. Indonesian warships were much in evidence.

In one *rumah makan* I met John, a photographer who had retired to West Timor from Darwin a few years before on the grounds that it was cheaper to live there. He showed me some of his photographs. I could see why he had retired early and needed to live cheaply. I might take photos like a chimpanzee let loose with a camera, but even I could see that they were terrible.

John commented on the profusion of X-rated cassettes you were entertained with in bemos. He said, 'On Sundays I come out of church after Mass. The bishop gets into his beautiful new Volvo while I and other poor peasants crush into a gaudy bemo. All the virtuous pillars of the church sit placidly, benign smiles lighting their faces while a foul rap song splits the air. Then the door of the bishop's car opens and out blasts the same song on his state-of-the-art stereo, much magnified and clearer.'

Another time I shared my table with a young Timorese. He asked me what I was doing in Timor. I said that I was waiting for the boat, then as we left the restaurant together, I noticed a ragged old man sitting on the pavement and leaning against the wall, his chin on his knees, seemingly asleep. He was not begging – I saw no beggars in Timor at all – but he looked in need.

'Do you think this poor old man wants something to eat?'

'Oh, yes, I think so,' he said.

'Would it be all right if I gave him some money?'

'Oh, yes indeed, I think so.'

'How much?'

He smiled, laid his hand gently on his chest, and said, 'It's up to you. From your heart.'

Bending down I slipped a couple of thousand into the old man's hand. Rupiahs, I mean, though I would have liked it to have been in dollars. (At the time, one Australian dollar fetched about fifteen hundred rupiah.)

At yet another eating establishment on the foreshore (I tried them all), I was joined by two of the help who settled themselves, uninvited, opposite me, and decided to practise their English. This happened often, and it always amused me. Can you imagine going into a restaurant in Australia and having the waiter fling himself casually into the chair next to you and start socialising?

It is called innocence, and it shows in their graffiti. Blazoned across a wall in Kupang someone had written in red paint their idea of a naughty word: 'PANTYHOSE'! This person obviously didn't understand the lyrics of the songs beating out of the bemo stereos.

Boarding time for the ship was six in the evening. The hotel driver took me down to the wharf in a van. I was ceremoniously installed in the front seat as though it was a place of honour. I would have preferred the relative safety of the back. In the front there were no windows, or at least nothing with which to wind them up. By the time I arrived at the ship, after a lengthy drive along the foreshore, I was looking wild and woolly. There were no seat-belts either – no such sissy things were used anywhere here.

Approaching the docks I looked down from the top of the hill and saw the huge white ship called the *Dobronsolo*; in front of it there was a large wharf enclosure packed solidly with people.

3 The *Dobronsolo*

It was one hell of a brawl to get aboard the ship through the mass of people, but the driver helped me struggle up the gangplank, and we reached the deck more or less still intact. My cabin had twin beds and its own bathroom but, as there was no other occupant, I had it to myself. I was the only western passenger aboard. Few Indonesian women travel alone, and as this was a Muslim country's ship it would be unthinkable for me to share my cabin with a man.

The *Dobronsolo*, built in Germany about five years before, was enormous, but not meant for the amount of people it was carrying – more than two thousand. I heard its capacity was only five hundred. There were a few first-class cabins and more second and third, but most passengers were travelling deck class, camping on the boards in a profusion of litter from the food supplies they brought with them or bought from the dining room. They also threw mountains of rubbish overboard, some of which landed on the roofs of the decks below, despite signs all over the ship exhorting people to keep it clean.

I explored the ship with difficulty. There was not

enough space to walk easily, and I could only pick my way gingerly between the hordes of bodies parked in every conceivable spot where it was possible to stake a claim to a piece of floor. Although deck class passengers were not supposed to be inside the ship, they had insinuated themselves in every nook or cranny – on the tops of stairways, on gangways, and all along the corridors to the cabins. The corridor outside my door was congested, and every time I ventured out I had to step over people sleeping, sitting, eating, chatting, doing crosswords, feeding babies. All doors leading onto the decks were locked except one, and it was not the one on my level. If there had been an accident, it would have been impossible for me to get out of my cabin and fight my way to a lifeboat – if there were any. And, if there were, there certainly would not have been enough. I could understand how two thousand passengers had drowned when one of the Pelni ships had sunk off the Sulawesi coast a few years ago.

I battled my way through – apologising at every point for stepping on people, who fortunately were very good-natured about me ploughing through what were now their bedrooms – to the top deck to watch the ship sail. An older Timorese woman, a teacher who spoke English well, joined me. It was just getting dark as the ship prepared to leave. Down on the wharf the sheds were festooned with garlands of coloured lights – a very pretty sight – for the country's fiftieth anniversary celebrations.

That first night we crossed the Suva Sea. It was rough and, as we tipped and swayed, I felt as though I was in a gigantic tea cup, being stirred by a giant spoon. I could not sleep for a long time, not because of the movement of the sea, I love that, but because the creaking sounds of the ship were new to me. Once I adjusted to them, I found them very soothing. I like the little groans and grunts a ship makes, almost like a living creature.

Looking out my two portholes in the morning, I could see that we were passing among many islands. The sky was overcast, but it cleared as we sailed along the coasts of Flores and Sumba. The sea, the colour of oiled gunmetal, had a slight swell, and an occasional foam-tipped wave broke its surface. The ship made little movement as it glided through the water. Far away below the engines throbbed, hummed and bumped, but the noise was not intrusive, and the gentle roll of the ship and the movement underfoot was pleasant.

I was very comfortable in my cabin. I watched the sea and had a restful time between meals. The first three classes of passengers ate in the enormous dining room, which was all red velvet and plush but had arctic air-conditioning. First-class passengers were allocated the premium position across the prow, right in front of a small stage on which, much to my surprise, a band of two boys and a girl sang and played as we ate our meals. Food was plentiful, as was the array of crockery and cutlery. The dinner plates were big white jobs with scalloped edges decorated with a double blue band and the ship's insignia. The stemmed drinking glasses were as big as vases and as difficult to drink from while trying to keep your left hand off the table, as is done in Islamic circles. The head waiter looked like a cuddlier version of President Sukarno – very stern and seriously aware of the importance of his position. He would come and fetch me if I didn't front for meals on time.

Everything about the table and the service was immaculate, but several waiters hovered the whole time watching everything I ate. I wondered if it was because there were only nine of us in first class, and they had nothing better to do, or because they were allowed to eat what we left. Knowing the way staff are treated in Indonesia, I had a horrible feeling that the latter was the reason for their keen interest. We were served rice from large buckets, soup from a giant tureen, and vegetables and meat – probably goat, very tough but tasty – from capacious bowls. This was followed by either a dreadfully uninteresting looking cake, or a dark pink blob of unknown aetiology that had been shaped in a jelly mould and was served sitting among an ooze of yellowish fluid. An object that would have looked more at home in a pathology laboratory than on a dining table. Greatly daring, I braved it. It tasted of nothing except rice flour.

The ship had no communal rooms. At one end of the dining room there was a lounge, but the off-duty staff were always comfortably established there with the lights turned low and the video on. And there was no room to sit on the deck, where every inch had been claimed as someone's territory and was jealously guarded against invasion. If so inclined you could entertain yourself with sweets and drinks at exorbitant prices from the small shop that opened spasmodically on the main deck. My ticket clearly spelled out that I was not permitted to gamble or sell myself, so there was little left to do except stay in my cabin.

At three every afternoon there would be a knock on my door. I would be confronted by a metal trolley as big as a freight car, bearing on its battered breast two Herculean tin kettles containing tea or *koppee*. I received of its bounty a glass of already heavily sweetened tea and two dry Sao biscuits, in their original plain and unadorned state, but wrapped into a neat parcel with toilet paper. I felt the shocked reaction of the waiter when I once made the mistake of taking this with my left hand. I had to keep reminding myself that I was back in a Muslim society.

The third evening the sea was almost flat, and a dark slaty blue. We passed Lombok and Bali in the night and all next morning ran along the coast of Java on a calm sea. In the afternoon we pulled into Surabaya, the second largest city in Indonesia and a major port. I did not go ashore; the hassle was too much to face and it was baking hot. I secured a bit of shade and watched the port and dockside activity from the deck, remembering the last time I entered Surabaya by sea – the ship, the crew and I had all been arrested, but that is another story.

The action in the port provided a premium diversion. A vast river of disembarking passengers streamed ashore, followed by a colossal pile of rubbish that was pushed or thrown off. The ship was then cleaned ready for the next onslaught of passengers. The harbour was crowded with ships either anchored or coming and going in all directions. A magnificent competitor in the Tall Ships Race from Bali to Jakarta, some of which I had seen in Darwin, came sailing majestically into harbour in full rig. She had bunting flying proudly from her three towering masts. It was a splendid sight. Then a white cruise ship, probably full of rich Americans doing their round the world thing, pulled in to drop anchor directly in front of the *Dobronsolo*.

Six hours later we were ready to sail for Jakarta. I watched a man on the wharf throw off the hawser – thick as an elephant's trunk – and we inched gradually away from the dock. The gap between the ship and the wharf slowly widened until there was a narrow chasm of water between them.

This was quickly filled as a farewell salvo of rubbish from above hit it – cartons, plastic bags, cigarette packets, drink tins. Even before this the harbour was horribly polluted, the water a thick brown sludge like boarding house pea soup. I would not have liked to fall in.

The *Dobronsolo* threaded her way out of harbour through everything imaginable in the way of shipping:

Bugis schooners – the ships of the Makassan pirates of old (or still) – wickedly elegant with their black billowing sails, wooden prahus, fishing boats, and navy ships. Two of the latter steamed past making fast time for the open sea, followed by the HMAS *Wollongong*. I heard that Australia and Indonesia were playing navy games together. The Australian crew were lined up in formation on the deck, as is navy custom when entering or leaving port, and looked most impressive in their tropical whites.

During the night I woke feeling decidedly squirmy in the stomach. The conviction that all was not well with my internal workings grew, until I was forced to get up and be thoroughly sick. I had food poisoning. Served me right, I had broken the rules. I had done a very silly thing and eaten an icecream from the shop. I had little sleep. The pills I dosed myself with came up again. I spent a good deal of the night in close contact with the porcelain fixtures in the bathroom, which was not the sort of porcelain I wanted to be in close contact with – staring at Mr Bristle's name in an Indonesian state of cleanliness is no way to spend an evening.

By morning I felt pretty much like death warmed up and failed to show for breakfast, a very bad sign for me and the cause of concern to President Sukarno who came to see where I was. All I wanted to do was lie down and groan but I had to disembark from the ship. We had reached Jakarta.

4 Sustenance and sleep

I had spent three nights on the *Dobronsolo* and had to spend a couple of hours more caught in the mad melee of pushing, shoving, scrambling disembarking passengers.

On dry land at last, I was set upon by the horde of taxi drivers laying in wait for prey on the wharf. They pounced on their hapless victims like the Assyrians 'come down like wolves on the fold'. Deciding from the look of me that I was bound to be stupid, they quoted prices four times the going rate and refused to use their meters. I told them to get lost and shared a semi-decrepit mini bus with a couple of Indonesians who were charged five thousand rupiah to my eighteen.

Jakarta! I remembered it well when I was hit by a sudden shock of tropical heat. But worse was the sight and smell of the smog that hung in a pungent, pinky-grey veil over everything and gave me the feeling that there was a constant barrier between me and the horizon.

It took an hour of rattling along in the bus, without the benefit of air-conditioning, to reach Jalan Jaksa in the centre of town where the traveller – as opposed to the tourist – hotels were, and by then I was feeling poorly.

The driver discovered I was an Australian and, not realising I understood some Indonesian, commented to the other passengers on the burning of the Australian flag. I hoped there would be no more trouble.

I lumped my bags into the hotel I had chosen from my guide book only to discover that it was full. After staggering up and down the street and in and out of several small hotels dragging my luggage behind me, I found a suitable one, the Djody Hotel, with a vacancy, but I had to pay for a double room.

By now I was desperately dehydrated, so I asked the receptionist for a drink. He sent me to the hotel cafe where I watched the girl attendant languidly making toast and thought frantically that getting a drink here could take hours. I left and, panting, went into a bar next door where an equally languid waitress went on an on about what I might want.

'Lemonade,' I squawked hoarsely.

'American or local?' she asked and then asked me to choose from a seemingly endless list of different grades, quality and brands.

I was in no state to contemplate these momentous choices. I kept thinking throughout her endless speech, I'm going to have to grab this woman by the throat and scream, 'Get me a drink. I am dying!'

After a long time, in which she seemed impervious to my panting and the sound of my dry mouth as I tried to talk, she brought me a glass of fluid. I fell on it. I never thought I'd be so glad to see lemonade.

I made it back to my room and collapsed on the bed. It was bliss to be supine. I slept for several hours, woke feeling better, and went to investigate the possibility of continuing on to Singapore by ship. It was virtually impossible to get through on the telephone in Jakarta; it used to be the norm to send a telegram or a taxi with a message instead. Luckily, I found a ship's agent in the same street as my hotel. He said he could arrange a ticket to the Indonesian island of Bintan, just south of Singapore in the Riau archipelago. Pelni did not go all the way to Singapore, but there were frequent ferries from Bintan.

I then gingerly tried an omelette and my stomach accepted it with glad cries. I was cured.

At the Djody Hotel I had a small room with a very high ceiling, from the top of which a dim light bulb gave out a depressing one-candle-power glow. I was thankful I had brought my portable emergency lighting system with me. It is only a lamp socket and bulb attached to a cord and plug, but it is worth its weight in cocky chaff as cheaper hotels rarely provide enough light for reading or writing or applying your lipstick.

The communal bathroom had grey cement walls and floor and a wooden barrel the size of a large beer keg in the corner. The barrel contained water and a dipper. A lone tap protruding from the wall was a sign that the pipes would produce no hot water. Confronted with a cold wash I always take a *mandi*, a Malay-type bath, using the dipper method. You plunge a container into a barrel of water and pour it over an area of your body, starting at your feet, then work slowly upwards, which is much better than subjecting the body to one sudden, all over, hearty blast from a cold shower.

My bed was only provided with a bottom sheet and so I produced my all-purpose sarong – which can be used as a dressing gown, bed cover, and any number of other things – turned it into a top sheet and promptly fell asleep. I always take one with me when I go travelling.

Next morning I went to the Jakarta museum. It was years since I had last been there, and I thought it vastly improved. The collection of South East Asian porcelain was marvellous – room after room filled with a stupendous amount of fine pieces in glass cases. The museum was housed in a wonderful white building that has a line of large columns across its facade making it reminiscent of a Greek temple and in front of them a mighty bronze statue of an elephant looks down from a commanding position on a plinth. Inside there are colonnaded slate and marble-paved paths between formal gardens studded with temple statues. Here you could sit and contemplate on stone seats. Among the exhibits were many massive old jars, some a good size in which to hide a body, if you run to that sort of thing – handy for Ali Baba – and much grand Dutch furniture. One china cabinet was almost as big as the place I live in. I had visited the museum in the early 1970s, when the building had been derelict. There had been few exhibits, the walls had been scarred with bullet and shell holes, and the fountain and fish pond had been waterless, filled instead with rubbish and dirt, the fish long gone.

I have been to Jakarta several times, but it seemed cleaner now than when I had last come a few years ago. There did not seem to be as many beggars and destitute people on the streets, but the pollution and smog was much worse. Away from the city centre were suburbs of affluent houses, originally built by the Dutch, where the Indonesian gentry and some expatriate workers lived. In these wealthy enclaves, two-storeyed mansions with high-walled gardens fronted clean, wide boulevards that now and then culminated in a well-tended park.

Near my hotel was a European-style restaurant that I took refuge in to escape the heat. Before long I was enjoying a large cold beer and proving great entertainment for a couple of Indonesian men sitting at the next table. The men asked the waiter to investigate me, and he came to my table and said, 'Are you married?'

I answered him – inventing a husband to suit the

occasion – and he said with surprise, 'Ah, you speak Indonesian!'

I explained that I had worked on the island of Sulawesi in the past and had visited Indonesia several times.

Apart from really cold beer, which was rare in Indonesia, the only recommendation I have for this tourist ambush was the delight of its English menu, which offered, among other things, a 'pickled union' – was that two drunks getting married?

On the day the ship sailed I spent the morning visiting the sailing ship wharves of the old port. It took an hour to get there in a taxi and when I got out I was grabbed by a boy who offered to show me the way to the *dhows* or prahus. He led me into a small alley lined by count-less tiny shops in front of which people sat mending and making things, then through a grotty area crammed and crowded with disintegrating shacks, which went all the way to the shore; the filth and litter in and on the water was revolting. Among the rubbish floated a legion of small sampans and dug-out canoes. We hired a sampan captained and crewed by an old woman in a conical straw hat. She paddled us across the sleazy water between a myriad of motley boats to where the sailing ships rode at anchor along the wharf. I walked down the line of them, a long hot walk. By this time the sun was fully out and it was blistering as well as humid.

When I reached the end, I was sweating and panting despite my umbrella. I do not usually walk about in the noonday sun, but the *dhows* were a superb sight, anchored, dozens of them, one after the other in a long row. They were built of wood in the style that has persisted for centuries, with their sails furled to the mast and their long pointed prows high overhanging the wharf below. They they looked like elegant, graceful sea birds resting on the water.

The wharves were covered with enormous piles of teak timber that had been used as ballast on ships coming in, as well as goods and supplies to go out. Because Indonesia consists of so many islands, a prodigious amount of shipping goes on around them and the *dhows* come and go continuously. There are also always enormous numbers of people travelling between islands – most of them trying to get on the same ship as I was, it seemed.

Boarding time for my ship, this time the *Rinjani*, was two in the afternoon and at exactly that time I was at the wharf ready to clock on. Outside the terminal building a huge throng of hopeful travellers stood or sat about. The baggage porter who had brought me this far from the taxi surveyed the scene, gave me his number, and retreated. An Indonesian youth, seeing that I looked a bit lost, came and told me that the boat had not yet arrived. 'It might be a while,' he added. I believed him. If the ship had to arrive and be unloaded, it was going to be a good while. I did what the others were doing, found a pozzie in the shade of the building, sat on the ground on a plastic bag and prepared for a long wait for our delinquent boat.

And it was a long wait! I sat there until half-past four and passed the time chatting to the various people who trickled up to visit me, the novelty in their midst. I was asked by a male student what I thought of Timor. I deflected this by saying I didn't discuss politics or religion as I was merely a tourist. Yesterday I had read in the Jakarta newspaper that two journalists had been jailed for thirty-two months for criticising the government. For once I was keeping my big mouth shut!

Suddenly there was movement at the station. My porter reappeared and we shuffled along among the great press of people that surged onto the wharf. Here chaos reigned, but I found myself, if not on the ship, at least in front of it where I was left to admire it at leisure.

29

Everyone else settled down patiently again, this time camping out in the blazing sun. The first-class passengers were provided with a sort of movable archway for shade, and I was pushed under this. Thank goodness for my solid-edged bag. I sat on that. I saw a young woman holding a small baby trying unsuccessfully to sit on her soft bag so I said, 'Here, sit on mine.' She accepted gratefully and we sat there, one either end like a pair of book ends, for about half an hour. Then the gangplank was lowered and four burly ship's officers mounted guard at its foot and tried to control the rush. They attempted to allow me to go up first. You really do get VIP treatment in first class if you are able to take advantage of it, but my porter had not reappeared so I had to let the multitude go past. Officers grabbed passengers and shoved them back shouting, 'Two by two!'

People tried to get a toe-hold on the gankplank by climbing over the sides or pushing around the officers. Even though the officers clutched, seized, shoved and man-handled everyone they could, there were not enough of them. What puzzled me was why there was such an extraordinary panic at all when boarding would have been so much easier if people had moved along quietly in line.

After the long hot struggle to get aboard it was a relief to be installed in my two-bed cabin. I was again the only occupant.

The *Rinjani* had come out of the same stable as the *Dobronsolo*, but a few years before it. Evidence of those extra years was everywhere – the carpets and floor tiles were worn threadbare by countless thousands of stamping feet, and the ship's fittings were beginning to fray or break. The attachment that was supposed to hold my porthole blind down had been broken off and not repaired, but an enterprising passenger had put a bit of twine through it to do the job. A great instance of making do.

Despite this my cabin was great. It had all the mod cons I needed, such as a colour television that worked and a hand-held shower with a bracket to hold it onto the wall. If I had known that this was the first of a long series of these implements I was to encounter, but the last bracket I was to find intact, I would have paused to admire it more, as there was nothing more difficult than taking a shower while holding said item in one hand.

Again I was the only Western passenger except for one very grotty back-packer I noticed coming aboard. He, she or it was travelling deck class and stood out like a sore thumb in the neat Indonesian crowd. It was again necessary to stay in my cabin, as this ship, although I had not thought it possible, was even more crowded than the *Dobronsolo*. You could not move on the deck. Passengers were packed on wall to wall. The *Rinjani* was grubbier too; in fact, it was unspeakably dirty and smelly, and once the passengers came aboard it got worse and worse. There were no stewards or cabin cleaners on these ships, but there were attempts to clean them in port after the departure of the passengers. I saw an employee ineffectively sweeping what was left of the carpet with a straw stick broom.

Even before we sailed there was a strong smell of vomit wafting about in the air. Investigating the ship, I started down the steps to the lowest deck, a large hold housing a huge crowd of people who were camped on the bare boards. I had only descended far enough to have my knees in the hold when I was assailed by a fetid stench that surged up in a wave and hit me – hot air reeking of vomit. I was nearly knocked off my perch. I know that nurses are supposed to get used this smell, but I can assure you that, although they may be able to stand it more than most folk, they never get to like it. I hastily back pedalled, thinking that to be stuck down there for two or three days must be like travelling in one of the old slave ships. Even before the ship had left the wharf, I saw people chundering over the side; even the rocking of the ship on her moorings was enough to set them off.

At our first port of call I went on deck when the passengers had gone ashore. The gangplanks had been pulled up to rest on the sides of the ship and the vessel was being cleaned. Men were out on the gangplanks scrubbing the sides of the ship with long-handled brooms. I wondered what they were doing until I realised that they were removing what had previously been stomach contents! Further down the ship men on scaffolding that had been swung over the side on ropes were using long-handled brooms to slosh white paint over the really difficult bits that wouldn't wash off.

The *Rinjani* was also a cockroach heaven. I saw one of the ship's crew using a big pump, like the ones council workers use to spray poison on bushes, to squirt liberal quantities of a chemical along the corridor past my cabin. Goodness knows what he was defiling me with. It did not seem to deter the cockroaches very much.

Next morning we anchored briefly off an island called Butok. There was no wharf so two long lighters were towed out by a tug, removing hundreds of passengers and, impossibly overloaded, taking them ashore. They then replaced the previous passengers with an equal number. Later that day we began passing through the hundreds of islands that make up the Riau archipelago. Only a few of them are inhabited and many are completely unexplored, but some are being developed by Singapore as resorts or for the exploitation of the oil and tin that has been found on them.

Because of our delayed sailing time, we did not arrive

at Kijang, the port on the south-eastern end of Bintan until midnight. Taking my chances with death I inserted myself in the swarm of pushing shoving people trying to get off the ship en masse. At the top of the gangplank I stood back to wait for the mob to clear a bit and was joined by a few Indonesians of like mind. Here we witnessed a horrible exhibition by the back-packer. Her voice determined her to be female and, judging by her accent, her nationality was French. She looked like nothing on earth and of no sex whatsoever – white, skinny, hairy legs with knobbly knees stuck into great lace-up boots; dirty baggy ragged shorts; unkempt ratty hair. Loaded down by her back-pack she was trying to join the multitude by shoving in from the side. She kept getting pushed back, got angry, lost her temper, and threw a wobbly. She shrieked and screamed abuse then, scrawny though she was, punched one bloke several times. A sort of 'Oooh' went up from the watching crowd and I went 'Oooh' with them because it was a disgraceful performance. I know how Indonesians view such behaviour and I was ashamed for her. She had let the side down. Foreigners have a hard enough time being accepted without someone giving us bad press like that. Eventually she managed to force herself into the crush. I hoped she would get trampled to death before she got to the bottom. I nearly did.

A young man approached me and said, 'I will be your porter,' and as I could not see an official porter, I agreed. He went off with my bigger bag and before I could stop him he also grabbed the bag I had not planned on being separated from, which contained valuables such as my travellers' cheques and visa card. (My cash and passport were on my body.) In the ensuing fracas, I lost him, but he was waiting at the bottom of the gangplank. Then he took off again, leaving me behind.

It was a dark, overcast night with no moon, and a few spots of rain touched my skin in the balmy air. I lifted my face to the moisture and sniffed the sweet-smelling air appreciatively as I sloshed along in the mud. It was evident that it had recently rained heavily; the ground underfoot was sticky with that sort of tenacious mud that claims your boots when you lift your feet. It was a long way across the wharf area to the gate in the high wire-fenced enclosure that led outside.

I struggled on in my porter's wake, falling further behind as I was swamped by the wedge of humanity trying to get through the gate. When I emerged from this stampede on the other side, I had lost him. I continued on up a long flight of steps to where a pack of mini buses waited, then up another of the same and yet another, but saw no sight of him. At the very top of the hill I began to worry. Had I lost everything I owned including most of my money? How could I have been so foolish! (It's easy, I answered myself. You have been practising.) I had not counted on its being so dark. There was no light at all except those on the gate and the buses. And my heart sank at the thought of being stuck on this tiny island, without even an American Express office to sort out my difficulties, or many facilities of any sort for that matter.

Mini-bus drivers kept trying to get my custom, asking me where I wanted to go. I couldn't make anyone understand my dilemma until finally one man told me to go back to see security at the entrance gate. It took me about half an hour to struggle back to the gate and I was feeling utterly hopeless when suddenly – the best sight I'd ever seen – there was my bag standing on the ground! I mounted guard over it until out of the mob rushed my porter with my other bag over his shoulder. He was so pleased to see me he almost threw his arms about me.

'Oh!' he said, 'I thought I'd lost you. 'I went to the security and I said, "I have lost one small foreign woman this big."'

He put his hand up to the middle of his chest, which was nowhere near my height. Why everyone always thinks I am small I don't know. After a joyous reunion we began labouring through the mud in search of a mini-bus to take me to town and a bed.

It was a long drive to the town. The port was on one end of the island and the town of Tanjung Pinang on the other, but I did not really care. I was damp, covered in mud and extremely weary. Even when I was once again gently pushed into the supposedly honoured seat in the front of the mini-bus, I was past considering the lack of seatbelts, road rules and other such niceties. And once again there was no window. Many people were packed into the back, along with my bag and its faithful attendant, and off we set.

We drove through a lovely cool night. The drizzle of rain increased to a downpour. The windscreen wipers did not work, so at what seemed like a thousand kilometres an hour, the driver hurtled along with his head out of the window. This was not relaxing for a front-seat passenger. After twenty kilometres or so we came to Tanjung Pinang and approached a hotel that looked like one of the horrendously expensive resorts in Singapore. Not for me.

At the next I was pushed in to ask for a quote. This one had all the signs of being an 'Arab on a Jaunt' hang out, so when the inflated prices were quoted to me in Singapore dollars, I gracefully declined. By then the driver and the rest of the patient passengers were probably wishing I would make up my mind and get off. I had begun to feel like Goldilocks. So I took the next one – a big old Chinese hotel that was reasonably priced and looked suitable, though at two in the morning any refuge was starting to look good. I did wonder at the amount of company around the brightly lit entrance hall where several men lounged about on divans, but the atmosphere was not unpleasant.

To reach this haven from the street my porter and I ascended a mountain of stairs that would have done a palace proud. I could see that the hotel, despite its present decline, must have been very grand in its day. At the top of the high approach was a lofty entrance that had corridors leading off it wider than most modern rooms and through which I trundled a great deal of the pesky mud that stuck to my boots. The room I was ushered into was clean and amply supplied with chunky old-fashioned furniture and was so big I could have held a dance in it.

Tanjung Pinang, the biggest town in the Riau archipelago, was not the collection of grass huts I had expected – it was pleasant, laid-back place, and I liked it. There were no big buildings, but it was a fair size and had some attractive houses on the foreshore, a few parks and gardens, and a couple of streets of small shops. But its main claims to fame were its two red light villages and its harbour, seething with sampans, freighters, wooden schooners and ships of all varieties. The town lay along the waterfront, and on one side the rickety wooden houses of the past still hung precariously over the sea on stilts.

There were no facilities to cash travellers' cheques because few western tourists ventured here. I changed some money privately by dipping into my secret well of American dollars. Checking the boat situation, I discovered that ships went only to Singapore and along the coast of Malaysia from here. I bought a ticket for a ship to Singapore departing in two days time then explored the interesting wharf area. There were two long jetties that joined across the end to form a rectangle. One side was for boats out to local islands and the other was for Singapore ships and ferries, and housed Customs and Immigration.

The Wisma Riau, where I was staying, was within walking distance of all the places I wanted to go. But the climate was so hot and sticky that it was like walking around in a sauna. I ate my meals either in the market or at the *rumah makan* in the basement of my hotel, which had adequate, cheap food but was totally devoid of ambience except for a fish tank containing one colossal silver fish.

The island of Penyenget lies so close off shore from Tanjung Pinang that its imposing great mosque can be seen clearly from the town. The Sultan of Riau was given the island as a wedding present and he built his palace on it and made it the capital of the kingdom. I learned that the island was historically interesting – it was covered with ruins and graveyards – and was accessible by boat for a few rupiah. So at the wharf I hopped down into what I thought was a sampan plying the route. A boat-load of well-dressed Indonesians smiled and made room for me. No one told me that they were going to a wedding and that this boat had been specially chartered for the purpose of transporting them hence. Arriving at the island the wedding guests and I climbed ashore. By this time I had received a warm invitation to join them, but I declined with thanks, feeling that I had already gate-crashed the party enough.

Both sides of the path leading up from the jetty were lined by houses of the village. Perched on stilts in the water, like wading birds, they were reached by narrow wooden gangplanks. At the top of the path I passed through an arched gateway with a big welcome sign over it, behind which loomed the large, ornate mosque. Its walls were painted a pale lemon, its minarets grass green. It was topped by shining gold domes and cupolas and surrounded by elegantly fenestrated and decorated walls.

The asphalt paths that wound around the island and through the villages on the water's edge were only big enough for bikes – there were no roads, or motor vehicles. The paths and gardens next to them were neat and manicured, their edges picked out by white painted stones. I followed the path that led past the mosque and away from the village; not much further on it went into the jungle and became a dirt track.

And what jungle it was! Quiet and eerie except for an occasional randy, determined rooster squawking and screeching, chasing a chook among the bushes. Further still into the jungle I found the sultan's palace, long deserted, but still a grand building in good repair. I climbed up to walk around the wide top of the high, mildew-stained wall that surrounded the palace. From this elevation I became even more aware of the exotic atmosphere, the oppressive stickiness of the air, and the intense quietness, broken now and then by an echoing bird call that only served to intensify the silence.

I walked for a long time along tiny dirt paths with dense ferns and foliage all around, stamping my shoes and hoping the snakes would hear me. It was lovely on foot in this haunting, leafy jungle but, boy, it was hot. Once the green gloom closed in on me there was not a breath of air; nothing stirred. I came to the next *kampong* of brightly painted houses that stood on poles in the shallows at the edge of the sea.

Looking at the water gently lapping between the houses I saw that the occupants disposed of their household rubbish by throwing it out of their conveniently glassless windows to wash in dirty heaps against the pylons.

I returned to the wharf exhausted after my walk, flopped down on a shaded bench on the pier and was soon chatting to the owner of one of the sampans moored there. Madi told me that the island was owned by one big extended family and that everyone who lived there was related. He said that although he belonged on Penyenget he had lived for many years in Bali but had returned because Bali became too worldly for him. I could empathise with this. It's too worldly for me too.

I hired Madi and his boat to take me back to Tanjung Pinang via the Snake River, which he assured me I must see. We put-putted across the bay, past Tanjung Pinang and along the coast of Bintan to the entrance of the Snake. Moving slowly to the throb of the engine, we were propelled gently up the river through impenetrable green mangroves that grew right down into the water. The reflections of the dense trees and foliage lay calmly on the glistening olive green water. I felt as though I was in a scene from an old Tarzan film.

We progressed several kilometres up-river. After spying a couple of shanty houses roosting shakily on stilts in the water near the mouth of the river, I saw no further signs of habitation until we came to a landing above which, high on a hill in solitary splendour among the prolific green of the jungle, stood a spectacular Chinese temple. A wide path and steps shaded by a pagoda-shaped roof had been built for the benefit of worshippers making the long climb to the temple. Panting and sweating I reached the top to view the excellent panorama beneath me – jungle undulating into the sparkling sea, hundreds of boats and, far below, away to the left, the town.

The temple was in three sections. First there was a breeze-way where an open-sided pagoda, flanked by two luxuriant palm trees, formed a frame through which you could admire the view. Then there were two inner courts with roofed pagodas, also open on all sides, that were hung with crimson Chinese banners, decorations and lanterns. Lamps of ruby oil glowed on the red lacquered altars and thin dark plumes of pungent smoke rose to heaven from lighted joss sticks stuck in large brass incense burners. I realised that the temple must have been put in this magnificent, but inaccessible, spot simply as a joyous celebration of the glory of nature.

The resident temple custodian, a tiny relic of a man shrivelled up like a dried leaf, pottered about and grinned at me toothlessly. I decided he would probably be on top of this hill forever because he would never be able to climb back up if he went down. But it was so peaceful and serene I felt it wouldn't be a bad place to stay for eternity, despite the murals around the walls that depicted the tortures of hell awaiting the wicked. I resolved to mend my ways.

That night I found a *pasar malam*, an open-air night market. Although only food was sold, the market covered two large blocks and was spectacular. On one block, the owners of the hundreds of tiny stalls cooked and served food which you ate parked on stools in front of tiny tables. On the second, the fruit market was a glorious kaleidoscope of colour as vendors stacked and piled exotic fruits in beautiful patterns.

It was only a short hop to the wharf to board the boat for Singapore, so I hired an ingenious contraption – a three-wheeled bicycle like a bicycle rickshaw, but instead of a people seat at the front it had a goods carrier made of metal like a mini trailer. Its owner pedalled my baggage out to the wharf.

He wanted to pedal me too, but I drew the line at that; it was quite bad enough making an exhibition of myself in the usual manner without sitting up in a tin tray, like a side of lamb in a baking dish, to be bumped over the wharf's lumpy planks. On the boat I commandeered a comfortable window seat in the cool air-conditioned open cabin. Right on departure time there were three long, loud blasts on the boat horn, an undecipherable message over the loud speaker, and we were Singapore bound.

5 Singapore sun

The 'fast ferry' from Bintan could not live up to its name, as the seas to Singapore were littered with islands, ships and boats through which it had to manoeuvre. Nevertheless the voyage only took two hours, plus twenty minutes waiting to get alongside the wharf in the heavy traffic. Once I had passed through Immigration – an easy task as I did not need a visa to enter Singapore and all the officials spoke English – it took a whole hour to get a taxi. An objectionable European man stood next to me and continually knocked Singapore. Roaring at a couple of locals he mistakenly thought were queue-jumping, he turned to me and said, 'I hate the arrogance of these people!'

The unmitigated gall of him! He was the arrogant one.

This was my eleventh visit to Singapore, the Lion City that had been merely a fishing village until Sir Stamford Raffles established it as a trading post. And it is still really just that; a big shopping centre, albeit a very prosperous one. It is the most affluent country in Asia after Japan and almost as crowded – this small island of six hundred and forty square kilometres, with its kilometre-long causeway that leads to Malaysia, has approximately 2,800,000 people crammed into it.

Seventy eight per cent are Chinese, fourteen per cent are Malay, seven per cent are Indian and one per cent are miscellaneous nationalities like European and Australian.

After all that waiting, the taxi driver did not know the whereabouts of the hotel I asked for and took the next person in line. Another driver, who had parked his car on a side road to have a rest, saw my rejection, walked over to me and said, 'Where do you want to go? You come along with me and I will help you find your place.'

I showed him the hotel name in my book. 'You come, you come,' he said, and after shovelling me into the car he took off, apologising all the way for the other driver's indifference.

The hotel was a real dump so I was not heartbroken to hear that it didn't have a vacant room. Three full or seedy hotels later, my driver suggested the Sun Sun, a nice old Chinese hotel. It was not ritzy, but it was squeaky clean, and it cost forty Singapore dollars after bargaining. Nothing was cheap in Singapore, except food, now that the Australian dollar was worth about the same as a Singapore one. A flight of narrow, polished wooden stairs between two shops in a busy street led up to the Sun Sun's foyer, which was always occupied by several old Chinese gentlemen who sat about on old brown leather couches in attitudes of indolent repose and greeted me courteously with bows and smiles every time I went in or out (which beats a couple of 'hotels' I have stayed at where the foyers were always full of lounging American sailors).

I liked my big room and its furnishings – two single iron beds standing on a red painted cement floor, a beautiful mid nineteenth century wooden table with turned legs, a bevelled and scalloped white marble top, and two nineteenth-century wooden cottage chairs. Antique dealers would have spilled blood to get their hands on this fine furniture that was slumming it in a hotel for budget travellers.

Two big wooden shuttered windows covered by wrought-iron grilles and curtains – no fly screens or glass – opened over the street two floors below. There was no wardrobe, merely one metal rack to hang my clothes on and another for towels. There was an old-fashioned wash-basin in the corner, and the bathroom, outside at the end of the open verandah, retained its original nineteenth-century fittings and plumbing. A toilet cistern, from which dangled an immense antique chain with a white porcelain knob, lurked way overhead close to the high ceiling. The drainage from the bathroom next door was channelled across the floor in a culvert so that it disappeared through a hole in the opposite wall. Goodness knows where it came to rest. You could stand in the shower and watch your neighbour's soapy water go past.

By the time I had organised the hotel it was dark and my stomach was insisting on attention. I found an outdoor Indian cafe nearby and, sitting down at a table on the edge of the street, ordered a curry, chappattis and beer, then relaxed in the cool of the evening. The waiter arrived with a big brown bottle of the amber fluid but, just as he whipped the top off, I remembered my financial state. I clapped my hand to my mouth and said, 'Oh! I have no money!'

The exchange rate at the terminal had been abysmal so, forgetting it was Sunday and expecting to find the money changers open in the city, I had only changed my remaining Indonesian rupiahs into cash. After paying the taxi I had a mere ten Singapore dollars left.

The Indian waiter, a nice old man, reassured me, 'Never mind, you change money across the street.'

I dashed over to the money changer's office he had pointed to, but it was closed. A man in the next shop directed me to another, which was also closed. Returning to the scene of the crime – chewing gum is illegal in this country, so what do they do to women who order food and can't pay? – I pleaded ignorance. 'Oh!' said the kindly waiter, 'Oh dear me.' Then he added, 'Never mind, how much you have?'

I told him I had ten dollars.

'Never mind, never mind, beer six, food three, only nine.'

Beaming with relief, this dear man consoled me. 'You see, you have eat, you have drunk, and you still have a dollar, you are all safe now.'

Drunk was nearly right. I had not anticipated a huge bottle of beer to myself.

Even though my hotel was almost inner city, once the traffic left the streets for the night my room was surprisingly quiet. First thing in the morning the song of the bul-bul and other birds came in through the open windows. Despite the fact that Singapore lost a lot of its charm and character as it became cleaner and more modern, it still has spectacular parks and gardens, exotic temples and magnificent old colonial buildings. I was pleased to see that some of the unique Chinese shop houses had been saved from the wrecker's ball and restored, and that pollution and traffic problems had been reduced by the curfews and penalties placed on traffic entering the city.

There are many things you can't do in Singapore besides chew gum: you can't spit or smoke in public places (thank goodness) or criticise the government. There was dissent, but I was told it was the custom to look under the table for a bugging device before you voice it.

Singapore is very tourist orientated, but the money changers do not open until noon, as I discovered to my distress the next day. I had no cash for breakfast. I set off early to the nearest change office, but it was hours and hours and miles and miles of walking later – I wore out a pair of shoes in Singapore, left them behind in a bin and bought another pair – before I got fed. The first money changer was closed, and the next, and I kept being directed further on until I ended up at the Raffles, Singapore's legendary colonial hotel. It had recently been extended and was even more stupendous than before, but the new part was in keeping with its original character – colonnades and arcades and shaded gardens with charming benches on which to enjoy the cool breeze off the sea. And a money changer who was open!

The inner beast appeased, I went looking for shipping companies who might supply me with a passage to Hong Kong. Asking directions to the first on my list, I was told how to get there via the MTR, the mass transit railway, an amazing creation. You descend into the realm of the troglodytes and there, in the refreshingly cool subterranean depths, you find massive expanses of shining terrazzo floors, gleaming escalators and sleek silver trains that zip you across town. Huge maps on the walls help you get your bearings and even I managed to find my way on and off a train completely unaided. I even arrived at my planned destination. I am always chuffed when I manage to master public transport. At home, on the rare occasion that I resort to it, I invariably mess up somehow by at least getting off at the wrong stop, if I do not actually get on the wrong bus going the wrong way.

After much wandering among towering skyscrapers

that looked much the same to me, I found the building I was looking for, to discover that the shipping firm had moved. The building's security man knew their new location and was most helpful. He said, 'You can walk. It's not far.'

Oh, yeah! One of those 'you can't miss it, it's only five minutes' spiels that I always fall for and vow each time I do that I never will again. I walked and walked and walked. Finding the street at last, I counted the numbers until I came upon a boarded up demolition site where the number I wanted should have been. I walked along the duck board in front of it to the next building. Its number was too high. I walked to the other end. Its number was too low. The ugly truth finally dawned that my building had been demolished. Seeing another shipping office nearby, I went in to ask the receptionist if she knew the location of the company I wanted. This obliging Indian woman, beautifully wrapped in a sky-blue sari, failed to find the address in the directory, so she phoned information for the number, called the firm, asked them where they were and wrote it down for me. She started giving me walking instructions, but by now I'd had quite enough walking to last me for the rest of my life – especially in hot, steamy Singapore. I took the piece of paper, expressed my gratitude, and said, 'I'll phone.'

I returned to the underground cool of the MTR, a relief after the heat outside, where I had seen public phones. I dialled the number. You get cut off automatically after a certain time if you don't keep feeding the machine ten-cent pieces and I ran out of patience and money waiting to be transferred to Mr Wu, who, I was informed, was the one person with shipping information. I gave up and decided to phone from the hotel.

When I did get Mr Wu, I found it had all been in vain.

They had no ship and no likelihood of one, not even a cruise ship, until February. And all the other places I rang gave me a similar answer.

Later I found myself near Bugis Street, the notorious gender-bending thoroughfare of the past. Nothing remained to remind me of its old lurid self when every night its sidewalk cafes had been crowded with exotic transvestites. It had not just been cleaned up, it had been sterilised! The entire street had been covered with glass, air-conditioned, revamped and turned into an upmarket shopping centre. The streets nearby were dotted with sidewalk cafes and tiny food stalls, packed with customers. In a small Muslim place I had a big heap of curried bean curd, rice and a Coke for one dollar fifty. The old man clearing the tables picked up my well-cleaned plate, laughed at the *nona* behind the counter, and said, 'She's a good eater.' He was surprised when I laughed. Tourists are not expected to understand Malay. I can follow it a little because it is similar to Indonesian, but in any case I am good at understanding anything to do with eating and food.

I gave up on the idea of finding a ship from Singapore to Hong Kong. Incredible though it seemed, considering the enormous amount of shipping movement between these two great ports, no passengers are carried. And I did not have time for a long wait. I had to get to Mongolia before the freezing winter set in. Reluctantly I booked a plane ticket to Hong Kong: Qantas, of course. I was told over the phone where to go to pay. 'You can't miss it,' a girlish voice uttered blithely, sounding the death knell for my ever finding it easily. 'It's just off Arab Street,' she chirruped.

Well, Arab Street was not easily missable but 'just off it' was. After several stops for directions I found the Sultan's Mosque – with its gold dome and vast prayer bell it was the impressive landmark of the area – and knew I was near. A charming young Chinese woman organised my ticket and then directed me to a bus that would take me to Chinatown, my next planned stop.

'When do I get off?'

She was tending the shrine of the house god that stood in a prominent place in the room, lighting a red lamp to place before it and making offerings of flowers and fruit.

'You can't miss it!'

No, of course not. But I almost did. When I thought I had gone far enough on the bus, I asked a young man if I was near. He said, 'Quick! This stop. This stop!' And I jumped off.

Chinatown had in the past been one of my favourite haunts in Singapore. The People's Shop had been the best and cheapest place to buy anything from arts and crafts to antiques but, sadly, I found it had become expensive.

Chinatown was evident only in some of the narrow back streets where there were still picturesque shops, temples, herbalists, calligraphers, food stalls and trishaws.

My plane was not leaving until three the next afternoon so in the morning I thought I would take a stroll to the museum. Of course, when I asked the hotel manager for directions, he uttered the usual words: 'You can't miss it.'

I walked right past the museum, went miles out of my way and got tired and sticky before I finally found it. Singapore is not the place for long walks in the sun! Housed in a grand colonial building, the museum had an exhibition of Imperial Chinese porcelains, mostly Ching. There was also an exhibition of memorabilia from the second world war. Neither exhibition held my interest for long.

I staggered back to my hotel, picked up my things and stood in the traffic for what seemed like hours in order to flag down a taxi. The hotel manager had said it was pointless phoning, but he'd kindly carried my bags down the stairs and put them on the street. The taxi driver was also a pleasant man who turned out to be a frustrated writer who longed to put into print the revelations of a taxi driver's life. His pride and joy and the love of his life was his Jack Russell terrier, which he had sent up from Melbourne as a puppy; the dog's photo, which I was handed to inspect and admire, graced the front of the cab.

The first night I was in Singapore there had been a tropical deluge and it had been overcast ever since, making the atmosphere even more humid and oppressive than usual. Now, as I neared the airport, the sky became blacker and blacker. Massive great banks of thunderous clouds rolled in, and the closer I came to getting on the plane the worse it became. My major fear of flying stems from the knowledge that taking off or landing in a storm is bad news. Curse the pilot who imparted that gem of wisdom to me.

Apart from my nervousness, luxurious Changi Airport was no hardship to wait in. You could camp there quite comfortably for a week, but not if you had to sustain yourself on their provisions. I had the most expensive drink of my life in the bar. A necessity as a pre-flight tranquilliser, it cost fifteen dollars. A sandwich with nothing but cheese, not even butter, cost seven, so I refrained from subscribing to this robbery. On the plane I was fed and watered free. A good meal, excellent wine and super service. The weather, however, was vile. I am sure the weather pixies turn on the worst they can expressly for White Knuckle Fliers.

The sky became increasingly dark and lowering.

I looked repeatedly out of the window and when I could no longer see the wing I really began to worry, as it was still supposed to be daylight. Little bumps became big bumps and the plane was shaken sideways and up and down. I vowed, yet again, that this was the very last time I was going to fly. After about three hours, when we had cleared most of the foul weather, the captain announced, 'Maybe you would like to know that we have just flown through the edge of Cyclone Nina and we now have clear weather ahead.' Pity he didn't tell us before we took off.

We landed just on dusk in Hong Kong. Customs and Immigration were a mere formality, and again a visa was not needed. Outside the air was tropically warm, moist and sticky, just like Singapore's, although this was autumn and it was usually cooler by this time.

In 1898, after the Opium Wars, China ceded Hong Kong to the British for ninety-nine years. As Britain had previously taken possession of the Kowloon Peninsula and the New Territories, this gave the British colony a total of 1070 square kilometres. At present Hong Kong's prosperous economy supports, mainly with trade and tourism, six million people, ninety-eight per cent of whom are Cantonese Chinese. It is a very westernised place and English is widely spoken.

While I was waiting for the airport bus to go to Kowloon, I was accosted by a respectable-looking young Chinese called Tonni who offered me a room in a guest house in the Chungking Mansions. I was heading there anyway, so I agreed.

My guest house was in fact around the corner from the Chungking Mansions, in a similarly monstrous rabbit warren of a building. Tonni led the way, dragging my bag behind him, through a long scruffy alley not more than three feet wide, full of rubbish and lined by the back doors of tiny shops. We came to a metal door in a wall which Tonni unlocked and we entered a corridor even scruffier than the lane. It was just like the Chungking.

It's nice to know some things never change. The dirty tiled passage finished at a truly grotty lift. Getting out on the twelfth floor, we came to another locked door which, when opened, led into a small foyer containing three more doors. Tonni opened one of these and presented me with my room. What a surprise after the grot outside. It was clean and well equipped, though not all the equipment was in working order, of course. The small room was dominated by an enormous double bed and a prodigious amount of cupboards occupied every other available space, all around on every wall, overhead and even over the mirror and dressing table, leaving just enough room to sidle around the bed and out the door.

When Tonni and I had been negotiating the price for this room I had asked if there was a bathroom. He told me that here was an outside bathroom.

I said, 'Shared, or in my room?'

He replied, 'Oh, no. Only yours, but outside room. Out the door.'

After he had left I discovered a door secreted among the cupboards on the side of the room. The air-conditioning in the room was great, but I was hot and I wanted a shower to cool off. I stripped down to my undies and pulled open the heavy metal door. The door opened inwards and I stepped out.

When Tonni had said outside, he had meant *outside*! I stood, in the warm open air of twilight, exposed to the entire population of Hong Kong if they had been so inclined to look. I, a self-confessed acrophobic, paralysed with shock and fright, was poised twelve floors up with nothing under my feet except a flimsy piece of metal. Then I saw the funny side of it. A few feet away in the building opposite, an old man was eating his dinner in front of the open window. He froze with his chopsticks halfway to his mouth and the hand holding them visibly shook. Male heads seemed to be popping up all over. I wondered if they paid higher rents for those properties that had the added attraction of the occasional unwary female tourist giving a free impromptu show.

The bathroom was a masterpiece of make do. The balcony was only three by four feet in size, just enough room to cram a small toilet on one end and allow space to walk out the door to get to it. The shower was merely a nozzle on a tube hung over the toilet. You had to stand sideways in front of the toilet, holding the shower with one hand and washing with the other. A microscopic basin was truly outside, resting against the exterior wall of the building next to the door. Entering the toilet cum shower, I thought, Help! On at least two sides I was on public display. But further exploration disclosed a con-certina door that afforded some privacy for most of my personal bits, only stopping short of my feet. That did not worry me. A voyeur would have to be very hard up or depraved to get off on the sight of my feet in the shower. Teeth or hand washing, however, had to be done in full view of the admiring or interested populace, because outside the protection of the loo's concertina door all that stood between me and the rest of Hong Kong were a few thin waist-high metal rails around the rest of the balcony. I looked at the other balconies opposite and above. Cluttered with rubbish, broken chairs, old boxes, they were petrifyingly unstable. One was hanging down on one side and in imminent danger of parting company with the wall. Whenever I went out on mine I wondered if this was the time it would collapse.

When I had recovered from the shock of my alfresco bathing, I went out to eat. It was only when I returned to the veritable maze of back streets in which I had taken up residence that I realised, with my defective sense of direction, I would need a miracle to make it back to my room. I had no way of identifying where my room was. Tonni had not given me a card, or a phone number, and my key tag had nothing written on it, not even a number.

At last I found the right alley – it was now pitch dark – and entered it praying that none of those sinister-looking doors would open to reveal Doctor Fu Man Chu or other notable villains. Clutching my handbag to my chest and expecting to be mugged at any minute, I stumbled over piles of junk and broken bits of guttering, and splashed in puddles of water. Several men brushed past me in the blackness. I made it to the end of the alley and came out into the tiny street, blessedly full of people, noise and lights. A few nasty moments followed – I couldn't find the metal door in the wall – until I remembered that it had been next to a girlie type bar, probably a brothel, where photos of half-naked, glamorous females were posted on the door. Outside the bar leaned an elderly Chinese girl with a hard face and a skin-tight red singlet and brief gold lurex shorts trying to lure passers-by. I was so glad to see her again I said, 'Hello.'

Home sweet home! I said to myself; followed by a lot of cursing as I wrestled with the lock on the metal door. The key didn't fit, but fortunately a group of Indian men coming out opened the door and I dashed in before it shut again.

Upstairs there was more trouble as the key would also not open the door into the foyer. I banged on the door until a woman opened it and let me in. Then more difficulties. In the foyer I was confronted by three identical doors and I had no idea which was mine. I tried one door. It opened. I crept in, found an unfamiliar, unmade bed and backed out hastily. By a process of elimination I worked out that as the woman had come out of the other door, the last one had to be mine.

In the bright light of morning I got the full impact of my surroundings and found it even harder to grasp that I had an outside bathroom on the twelfth floor of a sky-scraper. The building continued on for several floors and was surrounded by many other tall buildings in the same scabby condition. The walls were stained with black scaly mould, and bamboo poles festooned with tatty clothes stuck out from every window, like ragged totem poles. Between my building and the next was an L-shaped space containing the most appalling mess. Rubbish, thrown from the windows above for years, had piled up in the space or had stuck on the walls, coming to rest on any-thing that protruded on the way down.

Among all this filth a seed had landed in a crevice, taken root and grown into a tree that, in a celebra-tion of life, had lifted its branches six feet towards the light. Here and there, other bits of greenery struggled to survive, a tribute to nature's tenacious determination to reclaim her rights.

That morning I found Tonni and changed my room for a single one. It was a little cheaper, although in Hong Kong, like Singapore, nothing is cheap except food. It is the dearest place in Asia after Japan. My new room had an inside bathroom, a phrase that had recently taken on new importance to me, and was as big as a decent-sized shoe box and about that shape, a tiny, narrow rectangle rather like a ship's cabin. Most of the room space was taken up by a single bed, past which I had to edge crab-like to gain access to the loo. It in turn had to be approached with an elaborate minuet – in sideways, turn to the front, turn sideways, sit. It was a novelty to have to sit sideways because there was not enough room to put my legs in front, but you wouldn't want to be in a hurry and have to perform this intricate courtship ritual.

As soon as I had moved house I sought the ship to Shanghai. Many travel offices advertised ferries – some even 'fairies' – to Canton, but the China Navigation Company exclusively handled the Shanghai boat. I was only offered a cabin in first class. But I agreed as it wasn't expensive. Then I discovered I needed a Chinese visa before I could buy a ticket. To lodge my application took the rest of the day. And it was refused! I had never been refused a visa before, and it was a blow to get knocked back. I did not know that the Chinese government was not allowing women who looked like I did into Beijing at this time because the Fourth International World Conference on Women was about to start. Later that day I saw the sort of women they were excluding featured on the television news. It was a bit of a worry that the staff in the visa office believed I looked like an agitator, a feminist, a lesbian, or all three.

I knew things had been going too well. I had found the shipping company and the Chinese embassy, both over on Hong Kong side, at the first try and had even managed to get to them by using the MTR – just like Singapore's only bigger – only going to only one place I didn't mean to.

Footsore, I went to Moonsky Travel, also known as Monkey Business, where, I had read, I could arrange a visa to Mongolia. I told them I couldn't even get into China. They said that I should not have put Beijing on my visa application, and to try again.

I went back to the Chinese embassy the next day at nine o'clock – the crack of dawn for me – heavily disguised with different clothes, heavy reading glasses, which made it difficult to walk about in – everything was distorted as though I was under water – and a changed hair style. I had hoped to mingle unnoticed among the crowd but, unlike the day before when the place had been packed, there were now few people in the big room, and I was plainly visible to the woman who had rejected me the day before. I tried not to get in the line of people she was attending, but I saw her look at me. I thought I was sprung. This time, however, I managed to pass official scrutiny and had no further trauma, except having to fork out one hundred and fifty Hong Kong dollars. I was told to return the next day for my visa.

The following day, expecting a heavy hand to descend on my shoulder and to be accused of fraud, I went to collect my visa. But all went well. I even got the multiple entry visa I had requested so that I could go in and out of Outer Mongolia. Now all I had to do was get a visa to go there. This proved very difficult. To travel independently you have to produce an invitation from a Mongolian. Given more time I could probably have got around this; there are ways. But in the end I paid an exorbitant price for Monkey Business, well named, to include me on one of their group visas.

Returning to Kowloon, I crossed Hong Kong Harbour – one of the world's most spectacular – in a quaint and cheap ferry that rejoiced in the name of *Celestial Star*. Although the harbour was still as beautiful and scenic as always, I was sad to see that the sky and the multi-coloured boat traffic, constantly criss-crossing the sparkling water, were now dimmed by a heavy fog of pollution.

That evening I went to the Temple Street night market where all of Hong Kong were out doing their thing. Hong Kong people come out in droves at night, as they do in Singapore, which is hardly surprising considering the climate during the day. I had been to Hong Kong six times before this visit and I had once worked here for a short time, but on this trip I decided that I liked Singapore better. Before it had been the other way around. Singapore now had more trees and greenery and the people seemed friendlier and more helpful. Everyone in Hong Kong was in such a hurry. But there were some great things to do there.

You could visit the outer islands where the pace was slower, or take one of the most beautiful walks in the world – a pilgrimage I have made each time I've visited Hong Kong – the promenade around Victoria Peak at sunset. You take the funicular railway to the very top of the island and stroll along the path that completely encircles it. As you go, millions of lights come on all over Hong Kong and Kowloon, firstly against the sunset, then against the black velvet night sky and the sea.

It had taken me five days to orchestrate my entry into China and Outer Mongolia and by the time I was set to go my feet were worn out. Travelling is very hard work! I had been forced to do a lot of walking; taxis wouldn't always take me where I wanted to go as some areas were restricted to them. I managed the MTR and the cross harbour ferries okay, but buses were a mystery to me at the best of times. But I did try. I boarded a bus in Kowloon and, completely lost, went on an impromptu tour of the resettlement areas, which have become great cement blocks of depressing slums.

Despite the affluence of Hong Kong, where Mercedes are almost as common as Holdens in Australia, I still saw beggars, though not as many as there used to be. Now the beggars are the old people, the saddest sight of all. It grieved me to think that these venerable ancients had needed to resort to the indignity of begging in the streets at the time in their lives when traditionally they should have occupied an honoured position in the family. In one tiny park I noticed a very old man, dressed in dark tattered rags and carrying a small bundle of his worldly possessions. I thought it strange that he was sipping from a fast food drink container until I realised that he was scavenging from the bins, drinking dregs from cups and going through packages for scraps of food. I saw him three more times but I never saw him beg. The next time he was fast asleep on one of the seats so I slipped some money under his hand.

Since I had arrived in Hong Kong the skies had been dull and threatening. Cyclone Nina was following me. The day I collected my ticket on the ship to Shanghai, the typhoon warning signal was hoisted. Wouldn't you know.

6 Slow boat to China

I had imagined the Hong Kong ship terminal to be a chaotic scene similar to the pandemonium in Indonesia. Far from it. I was deposited by a taxi at the entrance of what looked like a ritzy hotel. Gliding my wheeled bags over the smooth terrazzo floor, a lovely sight for a wheelie, I progressed to a lift that zipped me up several floors and deposited me into the huge air-conditioned haven that was the departure lounge.

Looking out through the glass walls, I saw ferries and ships coming and going in all directions. The English announcements babbling from the loudspeakers were incomprehensible. I asked an official for directions, and he told me my ship would leave in an hour and showed me where to wait. I stationed myself next to some Chinese men whom I had ascertained were also going to Shanghai, and kept my eye on them.

Eventually one of the men said to me, 'Okay, we go now.'

And we went. We walked down a ramp in an orderly manner and onto a ferry the same as those that plough through the harbour to the outer islands. I thought that either I was on the wrong boat or this Shanghai ship had been vastly overrated. Three days in this tub? Heavens!

But the ferry only took us the first leg of our voyage, a forty-five minute chug around the harbour to where the ship, *Hai Sing*, reassuringly big and smart, majestically rode the waves at anchor. The Chinese, realising that I had thought the ferry was our transport to Shanghai, were still laughing days later.

To board the *Hai Sing* passengers had to negotiate a landing platform that rose and fell at least three feet on each wave. Two officers stood on either side of the platform, took hold of us one at a time and shunted us across to the other side, where we were grabbed by two others. We were caught, fielded and passed on, rather like sheep being run through a dip. All that was needed was a cattle prod.

The good ship *Hai Sing* belongs to mainland China, not Hong Kong, so the crew were from China, as were most of the passengers, and not much English was spoken. When I issued forth from my cabin after dumping my things, I met a young woman steward who greeted me with what I think were her only words of English, 'The bar is upstairs.' Did I have Australian written all over me, or was this the general view of foreigners: always panting for a drink? I obligingly bought a San Miguel beer which, at one dollar a can, sealed my good opinion of Chinese ships.

Fanned by a cool breeze, I reclined in a deck chair with my drink and watched the skyscrapers of Hong Kong Island slowly slide by. They looked as though a giant child had planted his Lego blocks on the shore, heaping and piling them at uneven heights one behind the other. Twenty minutes later we stopped, a boat came alongside and took off the pilot and we were away, slipping among numerous islands, bound for the South

China Sea which was, when we reached it, as calm as bath water.

The *Hai Sing*, I was delighted to discover, was a far cry from the Pelni ships. Everyone had a cabin and a bunk, there was no deck class, and the ship was clean and orderly. My ticket warned me that I must 'Adhere to public order – to protect the safety and "intersets" of passengers, each passenger shall adhere to the safe regulation and public order. The master is entitled to enforce anyone who are in breach of the provisions or don't obey the *persuation*.' I was 'persuated'. What was the alternative after such a grim warning? Flogging before the mast? Leg irons and chains?

Built in China in the fifties, the *Hai Sing* was furnished in late Art Deco style, with wood panelling and wooden bulkheads and doors. It had a big, quiet, comfortable lounge sporting, in pride of place, a grand piano. If this instrument had been on a Pelni ship, someone would have been sleeping in it. The piano had a fitted orange velvet cover trimmed with squashed-caterpillar green silk tassels. This decorator's nightmare was placed against grass-green velvet curtains draped with red banners and surrounded by pink and red floral armchairs and lounges. The dance floor had an immense mirrored ball suspended over its centre, as well as flashing coloured spotlights. The bar adjoined the lounge, and the dining room was one deck down. The ship carried about one hundred passengers and, strangely for a communist country, they were divided into lots of different classes. There was even one class higher than first, deluxe, but that was as far into the rarefied strata as you could go. So much for all their propaganda about China, the Great Classless Society. I never saw such blatant class distinction as in proudly communist China.

My single cabin and attached bathroom, with original

fittings and furnishings from the 1950s, was extremely comfortable, despite the raucous Chinese singing that came uninvited through the loud speaker on the wall, and sounded like someone was standing on the cat's tail.

There was no chance of missing my dinner. Three of the staff came knocking on my door to herd me to the fodder. In the dining room I sat down at a table with a couple of other westerners, but was hastily moved with profuse apologies – they were Z class, or worse. I was then steered to a large round table that bore a sign declaring it to be 'first class only'. There were seven of us: six Chinese and me. Only chopsticks were provided for the ingestion of the nutrients, and my table companions watched with interest to see how I coped, hoping, no doubt, that I'd botch it completely. I did not disappoint them. I made a terrible mess, but was relieved to see that they did too. Shanghai food is greasy. Even the rice was oily, and being watched made me nervous. I picked my chopsticks up by the wrong end, took a load of food, and spilled the lot. Realising my mistake, I took hold of the other end, but that was wet and greasy and I flipped the chopsticks over, spraying rice everywhere. The audience was delighted. They had expected the barbarian to be a pig and I fulfilled all their hopes.

Looking around the table I was glad I didn't have to do the washing up. Each person had ten dishes. Watching the others to see what they did, I followed suit. I chose three dishes of meat, chicken, fish or vegetables from the menu, then helped myself to rice, soup and fruit from huge communal bowls. Half-filling my bowl with boiled white rice, I took pieces from the dishes surrounding me, poised them over my rice bowl and then whipped them into my mouth and, with luck, not on the tablecloth. Some of the descriptions on the English translation of the menu were a trifle vague. One item offered was 'chicken left in dregs of wine'. Sounds nasty, but it probably meant marinated.

Up on deck later, I leaned over the bow, watching the green and white flecked wake froth away from the impact of the ship. Heavy, threatening clouds hung low over the west, possibly the edge of Nina still dogging me. The sinking sun caught the dark grey clouds from behind, turning their summits flamingo pink and sketching pale apricot streaks across their centres. The golden rays from the disappearing sun spread out fan-like from the horizon to mid sky. The illusion was like those in biblical pictures that depicted Moses, or a similar heavy, being addressed by God. I walked to the other side of the ship where I watched a daffodil-yellow full moon rising in a dove-grey sky. The light of the moon slowly formed a gilded path along the dark green sea. Then a thunderstorm loomed among the black clouds to the west, streaking them with flashes of spectacular lightning like silver wire.

It was the Moon, or Lantern, Festival, the fifteenth day of the eighth month of the Chinese calender. On this day of the full moon, you must eat moon cakes in order to gain good fortune. I found it was more like gaining indigestion – the cakes were heavy and, to my palate, tasteless. At dinner one of my companions, Mr Wong, an elderly Chinese businessman, had asked me to go to the party in the lounge that night to honour the Moon Festival. I agreed.

The festival is six hundred years old and supposedly dates from the Chinese peasants' revolt against their Mongol rulers, which eventually led to the downfall of the Yuan dynasty. The revolt organisers hid messages in cakes shaped like the full moon and lit lanterns as a signal to start the ruckus.

Arriving at the party, I found prizes proudly displayed

on the grand piano, which was stripped of its orange petticoat and ready for action – boxes of cigarettes, biscuits and edible Chinese delicacies like dried salted plums. I said, 'I never win anything, but I bet I get the cigarettes this time.'

We had moon cakes, pickled pea-pods, peanuts, jasmine tea, games, dancing, and Japan's revenge on the west – karaoke. The Chinese have no inhibitions about microphones. Give them one and they are away; talking, singing, performing, you can't get it off them. All the staff took part. One steward played the violin, another sang, and they all danced. I was seated with the only non-Chinese on board – a young American boy, a Japanese student and an American brother and sister – in a conspicuous place in the front. The show was conducted entirely in Chinese, so I didn't follow much. Then the stewards and stewardesses danced together, or with any passenger they could persuade to get off their seats. The foreigners who danced unwittingly provided a floor show for the seated Chinese. I danced with one of the passengers, a tall young Chinese man who danced well. We even did some rock and roll, aided and abetted by the ship, but we did not speak. When my silent partner had enough of dancing, he turned and walked off the floor, expecting me to follow. Nearing the seats he said, and I think this was the sum of his English repertoire, 'You sit,' and left me. I sat!

I danced with him several times and with some of the stewards, and each time I finished I received a round of applause. Marvellous, I thought. I've made it onto the stage at last. I even won a prize for my dancing. It was, yes, for the world's premier, militant anti-smoking activist, a carton of cigarettes.

During the evening I had a slight communication problem with the waiter. I asked him for a beer and he said, 'Come with me,' or something like it. I followed him out, thinking maybe I had to buy it at the bar, but he took me by the hand and led me to the toilet. No one else had drunk anything but tea so far and I began to wonder if I had committed some awful social gaffe. Maybe curses fell on those who polluted the Moon Festival with the demon drink.

The festivities started early and dead on half-past nine an announcement was made that shot all the Chinese to their feet as though their seats were electrified and someone had thrown the switch. The room cleared in three seconds flat. We aliens, not being in the habit of leaving parties so early and with such unseemly haste, sat on, wondering if the ship was sinking. Perhaps the announcement had been 'abandon ship'. Were they all in the lifeboats by now?

The crowd didn't return, so we moved to the bar. The first thing I learned in China was how to say 'beer' in Mandarin. The second thing was that you don't put the loo paper in the obvious place, but in the bucket alongside it, which the steward emptied twice a day.

I went to bed with my porthole open. Looking out I could see the reflection of the moon lying on the calm sea, and the bobbing lights of nearby fishing boats. I went to sleep with the moonlight and a balmy breeze on my face, thinking that this beat a jumbo jet any day.

I woke early, opened my eyes to a dull pre-dawn and watched the first lemony streaks of light colour the grey sky.

The day started with Chinese breakfast – a watery rice porridge, a kind of gruesome gruel, followed by a dry tasteless sort of bread roll that was a cross between a dumpling and a scone. Everyone else drank the gruel from their bowls, so I did the same, just a sip at a time. Drinking from a bowl felt strange, as though I was

69

licking my plate. I was wearing black silk slacks and a blue over-blouse with a high mandarin collar. Mr Wong said, 'You look half and half. Half Chinese – Ching dynasty – half Australian. But your look and manner and style are all Ching, you know, before the revolution.' No wonder the Dragon Lady, Madame Pu, glared at me across the table. She looked like a communist official, and I don't think she approved of me. I could imagine her having been the tough boss of a red army brigade during the revolution. She talked almost non stop to Mr Wong, in what sounded like a constant argument. Although she spoke no English, she made it clear that she thought I should sit with the other foreigners and not pollute her table.

Somewhere in the course of that day the sea changed its name to the East China Sea. We passed some small rugged islands but must have kept fairly close to the shore as there were always fishing boats nearby. The ship was very stable, and I could only notice the swell by the bobbing of other boats.

At breakfast the next day I discovered that the cooks had made an attempt to provide western-inspired food for the non-Chinese. But I had to wait for this delicacy, while everyone else chomped away at the Chinese edition. When my rations finally arrived, they consisted of two boiled eggs and a very thin, very dry, very strange omelette stuck between three slices of emaciated dry toast. And as a special concession – coffee. After watching me struggle with chopsticks for the last two days, the waiter produced a knife and fork to deal with the soft boiled eggs. A silent comment on my performance with chopsticks? I had decided that chopsticks were invented during a famine to slow down the consumption of food. It certainly did with me. I used the spoon from my coffee cup to eat my eggs. The rest I either had to eat one dry slice at a time or pick up all three together in my hand. Not elegant at any time but worse here, as one thing you don't do when eating Chinese-style is pick food up with your hands. The Chinese think westerners are absolutely barbaric the way we shovel our toast into our mouths with our fists.

As we progressed further north the weather became cooler and the sky more grey and cloudy. The sea continued to be dotted with islands, some appearing uninhabited, mere rocks protruding from the sea.

That night the foreigners karaoked in the lounge with a few extroverted Chinese. I watched. My singing was bad enough without compounding it with a microphone. Mr Wong came and sang 'Way down upon the Swannee River' to me. I said, 'Stephen Foster.' And he told me all about him. Then about himself. I seemed to have won a heart, but he wasn't Mr Right. His story was sad, but fascinating. As a young man in China he had qualified as an engineer. During the Cultural Revolution his wife had been killed by red guards and he had spent four years in gaol. Later, feeling all hope was gone from his life, he tried to kill himself three times. He then decided to live. Escaping to Hong Kong at the age of forty with twenty dollars in his pocket, he started working as a labourer. He was now seventy, the managing director of his own firm, and worth over twenty million dollars.

Mr Wong was a great talker, rattling on like a machine gun, staccato, loud, non-stop. His English was good, but difficult to follow at first because of his peculiar pronunciation. He looked like an amiable koala bear. There was no discontent in his face – all the lines in it went up, not down – and when he smiled his funny features were illuminated into pure geniality.

On the third evening the sea was completely calm and the light brown colour of a river in muddy flood as we came in close to the coast of China. From a long way out we could see a bright light which, I was told, was the light from the Shanghai Tower.

The ship dropped anchor off the entrance to the Huangpu River, on which Shanghai lies. We could see the lights of the city. We had arrived in China!

7 Shanghai sortie

Situated in Eastern Asia on the western coast of the Pacific Ocean, China covers an area of 9.6 million square kilometres, and has a sea territory of 6536 islands. It is the most populous nation on earth, with more than a billion people from fifty-six ethnic groups. The third largest country in the world after Russia and Canada, China measures roughly five thousand kilometres from east to west and five and a half from north to south. It contains four hundred and fifty cities. Shanghai, which translated literally means 'above the sea', is a separate municipality directly under the control of the central Beijing government and has a population of 12.6 million. It is China's biggest city and has the country's most important port and one of the world's largest. Two thousand ocean-going ships and fifteen thousand river steamers load and unload here every year.

Just before dawn next morning we moved slowly up the river. When light came I could see that the river was wide and mud coloured and that countless sampans, junks and landing barges carrying loads of sand, soil or gravel moved along it. Huge container ships were tied at the wharfs next to great rusting decrepit hulks. In the first grey light of dawn a stream of fishing boats passed on their way out to sea. None of the ships were smart or painted; even the couple of navy ships I saw looked old and drab. At first the foreshore presented nothing but a forest of cranes and chimneys, but these eventually gave way to dreary square blocks of buildings, unattractive and utilitarian.

All available land was built on right to the water's edge, and there was only an occasional lonely tree. The city looked dreary and industrialised from the water.

We had to wait until nine o'clock to go ashore because that was when the bureaucrats started work. Down on the pier we struggled over uneven wooden planks for about a mile before we reached the Customs and Immigration shed. There are no porters here. Capitalists carry their own bags, first class or not! Customs clearance was a mere wave of the hand for me, although the Chinese did not seem to be faring as well. Immigration was also easy, if slow, but the form that said 'You should go through the registration of stay after arriving your place' took me a while to work out.

A waiting taxi took me from the docks. It stopped soon after, right in the middle of a narrow busy street, so that the driver could get out and make a phone call. In the front seat of the taxi a clear moulded plastic igloo protected the driver on three sides. I noticed a wonderful coloured picture of a bedroom stuck to the back of the seat. I assumed it was an advertisement for a hotel.

'Take me there, please,' I said, pointing to it.

I was taken to a furniture shop. It was very nice, but I decided not to camp there and, amending my instructions, finally found one of the few moderately priced hotels in Shanghai, the Pu Jiang.

It was still early and I had to sit in the hotel foyer for

an hour until a room was available. This seemed to be
the only way to get a room in the cheaper hotels, as
they are constantly booked out in expensive Shanghai.
Foreigners are restricted to the use of certain government-
owned hotels. Other hotels cannot accept anyone except
Chinese. The only room I could get was one with four
beds. I was told I had to share – the room, not the bed
with any luck.

The Pu Jiang was originally the New Astor, the first
hotel the British built when they came to Shanghai to
establish their trading post. Situated at the end of the
Bund, Shanghai's famous water-front street, it must have
been superb in its heyday. Wide curved marble staircases
graced the inside of the building and the staircase at the
entrance was the width of a fallow paddock. Three fabulous chandeliers hung in the foyer. They were the size of
tree houses, so big you could live in them, but they were
now badly in need of a duster. Only the side wing of the
building was still used as a hotel. The main part, behind
the imposing front steps, had become the heavily guarded
Shanghai Stock Exchange.

It was a hike to get from the stairs to my room. I practically needed a cut lunch to make it. Walking on floors of
polished wooden planks uneven with age, through the
maze of wide corridors that were panelled with dark, patterned wood, I felt as though I was strolling the corridors
of an old English boys' school.

Lying on the bed in my room at last, I gazed up at a
ceiling twenty feet away. Through the open windows I
could hear the resonant hooting of ship horns, which continued long into the night, and see the river traffic. For
relaxation and a good laugh, I read the hotel regulations:

> Guests must prove their identity with papers and tell
> the reason for lodging there.

No guest is allowed to up anyone for the night.
No birds, domestic animals, or other unsnairy articles
are allowed to be brought into the hotel.
No inflammable, explosive, poisonous, radioactive, or
dangerous articles are allowed. Nor burning of articles,
letting off firecrackers and fireworks permitted.
It is impermissible to install electris stoves and
equipment.
Strictly forbid any illegal and criminal activities such as
fighting, gambling, drug taking, prostitution.
No guest should put up or circulate salacious books,
pictures, photos, or recordings and videos.
Any drinking excessively, making great noise or playing
loudly in hotel is forbidden.
Those who violate will be punished by the public
security organs.

That didn't leave many enjoyable things to do, so I
went in search of China International Travel Service
(CITS) – the service part is a gross misnomer – to book
a train to Beijing. CITS was the government travel
organisation. Its sole function was to help tourists with
bookings and supply information about travel, but I had
heard that they were never much help. I walked over
the bridge and past Huangpu, the park that once bore
the infamous sign: 'No dogs or Chinese allowed'. Soon
I arrived at the fabulous old European and British buildings that form a tall line along the Bund. They were a
melange of shapes and styles – European, Neo-Classical,
1920s New York, Egyptian Monumental – and many
incorporated the fenestrations, cupolas and columns
fashionable in the Victorian era. Seeing them through
sepia-coloured smog, I felt as though I had stepped into
an old photo. During the Cultural Revolution in 1967,
many of these beautiful buildings had been defaced,

damaged or had their stained-glass windows and decorations painted over.

On the river side a promenade travelled the length of the Bund as far as Huangpu Park. It was dotted with small eating stalls and photo booths that catered to the Chinese tourists who came there in droves to have their pictures taken.

Because of its long history of foreign influence, Shanghai is more cosmopolitan and westernised than the rest of China, and its people more sophisticated. Its European legacy includes five operating Christian churches that play to capacity audiences every Sunday. Before the revolution Shanghai had been an iniquitous, wickedly glamorous boom town known as the Paris of the East, along with other less salubrious names like the Whore of China. Shanghai had started as a British concession that became an international settlement which lasted until the 1940s. Each sector had its own laws and taxes. The port had existed on trade in tea and silk, but it had been the opium which the British used as foreign exchange that had made it flourish.

Its Western skyline remains, but most of the foreigners – European and American fortune hunters, social climbers, adventurers and sinners – have long gone. But the foreign population is slowly drifting back as economic good times come again to China.

Shanghai is a great industrial centre with a higher standard of living than the rest of the country. But the environment is ravaged and abused. More than ten thousand factories belch smoke and gas throughout the city. Heavy smog, a grey combination of pollution and cloud, hangs over everything.

Among the massive manufacturing output in Shanghai are items now obsolete in the West – spittoons, chamber pots, treadle sewing machines and steam engines. The latter, first designed and made in China in 600 AD, are still hammered out by hand. The Chinese were also the first to make steel, paper, crossbows, umbrellas, porcelain and kites, and they printed the first book on movable type. They first made parachutes in 1192 AD, although the theory had been around since 550 BC when condemned prisoners were chucked off parapets tied to bamboo contraptions in order to test drive them.

I found CITS after much trouble. The information in my guide book, although it was the latest edition, was already out of date. And the prices for everything were more than double those quoted. China was on the move – fast! The Peace Hotel, the former Cathay, where the CITS office was alleged to have been, was another august colonial hotel which reposed behind the wrought-iron gates and grand doors of its front entrance. Under its massive light fittings and multi-coloured glass sky lights, Noel Coward wrote *Private Lives*.

After waiting for the CITS staff to return from their customary two-hour lunch, I was told that that office no longer sold train tickets, only those for the plane. I was directed to another CITS office where I stood for ages before the desk of a woman who carried on a private conversation with a colleague across the room while studiously ignoring me. When she finally condescended to acknowledge my presence, it was to tell me that there were no train tickets to Beijing. I persisted, refusing to go away until she finally produced a ticket in an off-hand manner. She could not have cared less where I went or how I got there as long as I stopped bothering her. Dragging information out of her, such as the train's departure time, was like pulling teeth. The next time I needed a train ticket I went directly to the train station and did better – even on the price. I visited the ever unhelpful CITS again before I left Shanghai to enquire about river steamers down the Yangtze. They knew nothing

I was to discover, from sad experience, that CITS only wanted you to fly, or go on a tour. Anything else did not bring in enough loot for them and was simply too much trouble. China's airline was called CAAC. Would you fly with something that sounds like you might step on it in the chook yard? Dissatisfied foreigners who have flown with them insist that the initials stand for China Airlines Always Crash. CAAC does have an appalling track record for losing planes. Definitely not for me!

I also discovered that the banks closed at midday for that two-hour lunch again. I hurried to make it in time. The first I tried was barricaded like Fort Knox. Its gate was guarded by a sentry with a huge gun. To gain admission you needed to insert your card in the slot provided. If you did not have a card, you did not get in the door. No soliciting of stray tourists for them. I wondered how they procured new accounts.

The Bank of China was not so particular about keeping the riff-raff out and allowed me to enter their hallowed halls unmolested. The bank was in a stately Victorian building with polished marble floors and great lofty ceilings. Down either side of a vast hall fifty tellers stared at each other across an open space as big as a football oval. Only one of this platoon was occupied – the traveller cheque fairy. Ten frantic foreigners were all trying to extract funds from him at the same time. It was nearing the magic stroke of twelve and maybe they feared turning into pumpkins or white mice.

One disgruntled traveller wrote that Chinese officials were always badly dressed, bad tempered and rigid, that train conductors were tyrants to everyone while security guards were harsh on their own people. A popular Chinese proverb says, 'We can always fool a foreigner.'

That says it all. You get the distinct feeling that they don't like you.

I wore out another pair of shoes walking in Shanghai, looking for places listed in my guide book. It's a funny thing that maps of cities always have streets marked as broad thoroughfares that go straight up and down. When you actually get to the streets they are usually narrow affairs that wander all over the place and are smothered in shops, people and bicycles. On all the streets in China I was assaulted by the sound of spitting and throat clearing. The spitting was bad enough, but the throat clearing and hawking, revoltingly juicy sounds, like a plunger clearing a septic tank, could be heard for miles and was absolutely stomach turning.

In my wanderings I came across a local Chinese cafe where I decided to eat lunch. On the wall was a large Chinese menu, but there were no English subtitles. I used the Look and Point system – see what the other diners have and point at what looks decent. I received a plate of goodies like spring rolls, I assumed, wrapped in edible rice paper. Closely watched by the staff and as many customers as could get a viewing position, I proceeded to eat a couple of the parcels before I discovered that the wrapping was real paper and not at all edible. No doubt the onlookers thought the foreigner quite mad.

My first night in Shanghai I ate in my hotel's restaurant. It was not cheap – a plate of fried rice cost thirteen dollars. I had the same meal later in a local cafe for a few cents. No wonder I dined in solitary splendour closely attended by a staff of eight. A waitress stood at my elbow and practically spoon-fed me, giving me a tiny bowl that she kept filling from a big bowl. She could have saved us both a lot of trouble by giving me the big bowl to begin with. It was a very uncomfortable meal. I had earlier had a six-dollar cup of coffee, and black at that, in the

Peace Hotel. I wondered where the legendary good cheap Chinese food was. Not in big hotels, that was obvious. I concluded, though, from the fascinated attention I received whenever I ate at small local places, that tourists must usually eat at the hotels they stay in. Probably because most of them are on package deals.

On the Bund the Colonel of finger lickin' fame had set up his shop. An enterprising Chinese soul had unashamedly installed an imitation, Shanghai Fried, right alongside it. On principle I chose to eat at the latter. Who would go to China to eat Kentucky Fried?

In Shanghai Fried big coloured pictures of food served as the menu on the wall, a boon for illiterate Look and Pointers. This tiny cafe was bursting with staff. Two girls were stationed behind the counter, another took the money, while yet another – whose function was obscure – stood at the door. I watched a man eating fried drumsticks with chopsticks, which was quite interesting. Then it was my turn to perform.

The four staff watched me closely, no doubt waiting for me to make a fool of myself with the chopsticks. I thought, I'll show them! and started off well. I could see they were impressed so I put a bit of a flourish into it and then, gaining confidence, really showed off by picking up my peas individually. Wow! They thought that was great! I almost received a round of applause. As my mother told me often, however, pride goes before a fall. I dropped the chopsticks and skittered peas all over the floor.

Eating was often an adventure. I frequently ordered something that was a surprise package when it arrived. I must have a faulty pointer. Once I asked for a dish that was translated as 'sliced potato' on the menu. In Hong Kongese or Indonesian this would be the local version of chip potatoes, and I eagerly anticipated some form of fried spud. But what was put before me was raw potato sliced as small as bean shoots. For once the menu had been accurate. But I had been emotionally prepared for chips and was hugely disappointed.

Shanghai traffic was terrifying. It came at you from all angles at a mad pace, with a wild cacophony of roars and rattles. Shanghai had more cars than anywhere else in China and the traffic didn't drive or ride on the side of the road to which I was accustomed. In this frantic tangle of transportation, I would make it half-way across the road and, pausing in the middle, think, You beaut, there's a blank space in front where I can cross. I would step into the road and suddenly the traffic would come roaring at me from behind. I was looking the wrong way and the charge of the light brigade was about to run me down! Even when I looked the right way, there would be cars driving on the wrong side of the road. You couldn't win. No one obeyed road rules, if there were any, and vehicles swerved all over the road.

Traffic raced through red lights and zoomed past policemen with their hands up for them to stop. I never expected to leave China alive.

Some streets were for bicycles only. Rounding a corner abruptly, I found myself in the middle of a wide road where, coming at me full pelt, pedalling like fiends incarnate and ringing their bells like loonies, was what looked like the entire Tour de France. Most streets don't have white lines down the middle, and bicycles bear down on you, wheeling and wobbling, from all angles. The poor defenceless pedestrian is the lowest order of life on the traffic pecking scale. It's up to him to get out of the way of danger. I concluded, after a few near death experiences, that pedestrian crossings were only there to give road users a target.

There was a congestion of pedestrians at crossings,

which, like animals at a waterhole, gave the hunter more chance of scoring a hit.

Footpaths, where it was necessary to push through dense crowds to survive, were not much better. People here told me that they find Shanghai unbearable because of the crowds and the noise. Nanjing Dong, the main shopping drag, was the equivalent of the Via Roma in Naples and even more expensive. Where were the super cheap items labelled 'Made In China' that you see everywhere in Australia? The prices were horrifying – two hundred dollars upwards for a pair of shoes, a cashmere coat for more than a thousand dollars. Where did the real people of China shop? But eventually I progressed to the end of the Bund and found the Chinese sector, where there were realistic prices. In a shoe shop I met two charming little gigglers who sold me a comfortable pair of leather shoes for six dollars. Months later this trusty footwear limped off the plane with me at Adelaide, and has been seconded to garden duty. I like to get my money's worth.

8 Magic

Each floor of my hotel had a room attendant established at a desk. The attendants' mission in life was to watch the goings on – or prevent them – and to be in charge of lots of rubber stamps. Everything got stamped. And the stamps were kept under lock and key in the desk. To get into your room initially you had to cough up fifty *yuan*, and the receipt they gave you at reception that proved you had paid. The room attendant would then take a key from the depths of her apparel, open a box on top of the desk and, removing a key, unlock the desk. The ritual would then progress – the removal of a key from a row of hooks inside the desk, the selection of the correct stamp, the painstaking stamping, copying and signing of the papers. China appeared to be strangling in red tape.

The room attendant was strategically positioned at the entrance to the floor between the lift and the stairs. A notice on the desk warned that the Public Security Bureau, the police, insisted that all visitors must be registered.

That's if a guest made it this far. Visitors could not pass

reception unless they registered in writing who they were, who they wanted to see, and why.

The first night at the Pu Jiang I was nearly asleep when the room attendant crashed through my door to install another resident, which completed our quota of four. At six in the morning the room attendant again charged in with a thermos of hot water for our morning tea. Sleep was impossible after this. Our room fairy was one of those souls with a complex – give them a little power and they turn into despots.

The second night, again after lights out, the attendant came in, all in a lather, because she had discovered I was in bed number three and my docket said bed number four. The beds were not numbered, and I couldn't read the docket, so how was I to know?

But she did, and it worried her no end. She was terribly put out that I had slept in the wrong bed up till now and insisted I move immediately into the bed next to it, my rightful place as ordained by the holy book of rules. I decided I liked it where I was. I gesticulated to her to change the bed number on my form. She refused and phoned the reception desk. I had to get dressed and go downstairs, fill out the official registration forms again and return with written proof that I was entitled to be in bed three.

My key even had to be exchanged for the correct one – despite the fact that all the keys to the room were the same, bearing only the number of the room on them. But this key had hung on a hook labelled Three, not Four, so I changed one key for another exactly the same just to keep this pernickety woman happy.

One of my room-mates was an Australian girl called Julia. She spoke fluent Chinese and was on her way back to Taiwan where she taught English, having been to Beijing to attend part of the International Women's

Conference. She said that the Tibetan delegates had been harassed, followed and persecuted. The Tibetans apparently invited trouble and violence in order to bring attention to their country's unlawful domination by China and their subsequent loss of freedom. Lectures given by Tibetans had been intentionally poorly housed to limit the numbers that could attend. In one case a fourteen foot-square room had hundreds squashed into it. Julia said that other than that there had not been many problems at the conference, and that it had been interesting.

Breakfast was provided in the Pu Jiang's restaurant. Weak coffee – an expensive and hard to find item in China – one egg, a sausage, and two small and strange-tasting pieces of faintly toasted bread without any embellishments. Each place setting had good quality silver-plated cutlery: knife, fork and butter knife. As there was never any butter, I wondered what I was supposed to do with the latter. The egg came almost raw. I don't mind a runny yolk, but these had runny whites, and little globs of clear albumen slid off when you tried to eat it. The sausage was half a skinny frankfurter. I left the table determined to get more food as soon as possible.

The biggest obstacle foreigners encounter in China is the language barrier. To find my way around town I would ask the hotel reception staff to write my destination in Chinese. In other situations I would use my Chinese phrase book and point to the word for what I wanted. China's official language, Mandarin, is based on the Beijing dialect, which I found almost impossible to master. Each word has many different meanings depending on the tone used to pronounce it, so when I learned a word and tried to say it, no one understood me. I am tone deaf, as proved by my awful singing. I only managed to master, hello, goodbye, no, yes, thank you and beer. And even these caused some people to fall down in hysterics, so goodness knows what I was really saying. But I did learn finger counting, a sort of numbers sign language, which was invaluable. For example, you put your two index fingers together crossed like an X for ten. Because I have a finger missing, I had an impediment in my speech, but I managed.

By means of my scrap of paper covered with Chinese characters, I navigated to the Friendship Shop, a massive, six-storeyed hulk of a building where the prices were anything but friendly. But the store was wonderful inside. It had escalators, lifts, air-conditioning, and a cast of thousands pretending to be shop assistants. Only tourists seemed to come here to gawk at the goods, and I never saw anyone hand over any shekels. By my standards the prices were outrageous, although some of the merchandise was very fine – huge carved jade figures and screens inlaid with mother of pearl and semi-precious stones.

Seeking a local market I had read about, I spotted a covered archway near the river and thought that was it. But it was a smelly fish market contained in an interesting old building with a colossal high-domed roof of glass. In the narrow aisles, on the floor, or on makeshift trestles were tubs of the famous hairy crabs – a local delicacy in season – as well as anything else that could be dragged from the ocean or river. The air was smelly, but it was not nauseating like the meat market that I wandered into next. My stomach turned. I did not enjoy the walk through there. I almost ran. Mutilated carcasses – some of them dogs, with their heads still attached – hung from hooks, while great chunks of bloody meat lay uncovered in old chipped enamel trays on wooden tables. A western meat inspector would have had a fit.

I wanted to buy a down coat for my trip to Mongolia and decided it would be easier to find the shop by taxi.

The driver was a smart, attractive young woman wearing a tight-fitting sleeveless black and white dress and white high-heeled shoes. She skilfully manoeuvred her beat up bomb through the horrendous traffic. All Shanghai taxis are red, but the price differs with the size – big cars cost more than Datsun 120Ys or Colts. Class distinction in taxis too! Drivers displayed a photo of themselves on the dashboard. After a while I noticed that in all the photos the men wore an identical navy blue suit, circa 1940. I decided it must be a communal affair supplied by the photographer.

Heading downtown we crossed the bridge that broached Huangpu Creek, an offshoot of the river. Alongside it a huge billboard featured the Marlboro man. In full living colour he galloped across the bridge sucking on his cigarette – looking very European and incongruous in China. There were also lurid, giant-sized movie posters of people inflicting mayhem on each other with various bloody implements, a strong indication of the Chinese preference for violent films. Demolition and construction was going on all over the city. I loved the bamboo scaffolding that was woven around buildings. It looked like an enormous shopping basket. I saw children being collected from school. You would not risk letting your one precious child loose alone in this traffic.

Downtown the taxi sat in a solid block of traffic, only inching forward occasionally. Drivers got frustrated in this melee and did the most amazing things. Policemen wearing olive-green trousers and pale-green shirts had to mount guard at traffic lights, otherwise no one would stop. It took an hour and five minutes to get to the locality I wanted, just two kilometres away from the hotel, and we still weren't at the shop. Finally I got out and walked. There were no street numbers displayed. It was difficult enough to get anyone to admit to one, let alone put it out the front. Clutching my piece of paper with the Chinese writing on it like a talisman, I went from door to door until finally someone confessed that their number was the one I sought. But the shop had moved!

I tried to hail another taxi to visit the Mandarin Gardens. I had never seen so many taxis in all my life and they were all full. As they were not all that cheap I concluded that the average person in China was not as poor as I had imagined, although Shanghai was not like the rest of the country. A motor-bike taxi came along and solicited my custom and I took it in desperation. It was an ordinary two-wheeled, two-stroke motor-bike but it had a contraption, of dubious stability, stuck precariously on the back in which you sat, open to the four winds. We had not gone far before my tiny canvas lid, the only protection I had from the elements, blew off and we had to stop to retrieve it. To restart the engine the driver heaved on a pull cord similar to that of a lawnmower. It certainly sounded like one. Off we went again. I anxiously watched the traffic looming at me from all sides, but we only had one accident and that was with a bicycle. Neither party was hurt and no one got upset. We passed down an immense street, flanked by two of the ugliest buildings I have ever seen, the parliament house and municipal chambers. They were new, huge and starkly hideous in the Soviet manner.

I spent half an hour on this motor-bike contrivance, and we slotted through the traffic where a taxi could not have gone. I would look at the openings between buses and trucks and think, There's no way he's going to fit through there, but he did, and he was pretty good at it too. But it was not all that good for the nerves.

The Yu Yuan, or Mandarin Gardens, which cover

20,000 square metres, were constructed for the private enjoyment of a wealthy Chinese noble family more than four hundred years ago. It is decorative and ornamental with its upswept roofs and it was the first Chinese-looking structure I had seen so far in China! It is blessed with a four hundred year old ginko tree and a two hundred year old magnolia. The south side was for women only, as in those days aristocratic women were kept out of sight of the masses. Standing on stilts in the middle of a lake is the original, ancient, five-sided Wuxingting Tea House, which could be reached via a quaint curved bridge.

On the lake a worker punted around in a small boat fishing out all the rubbish that the locals had chucked in for the amusement and edification of the resident swans and gold-fish. The Temple of the Town Gods is also incorporated in the complex. This is an imposing edifice with guardian lions and dogs of Fu flanking its entrance, and huge curling corners on the tiled roofs. Much incense and singing, chanting, clashing and clanging of gongs and cymbals poured from inside and it seemed as if they were up to something interesting in there, but I could only peer through the barricaded door as I was not allowed inside.

Many of the buildings in the gardens had been converted to big shops with big prices. They were full of tourists and tourist rubbish. This was not my scene. I left and wandered happily through the surrounding maze of narrow, rough cobbled lanes and alleys that all had open drains and rows of tiny tumbledown houses with washing hanging from the windows. These vivid back streets, only big enough for walking in, were a remnant of old China and the sort of thing I enjoy. A barber wielding a cut-throat razor did his barbering on the street – a real close shave – using a superb antique barber's chair. There were minute shops, improvised stalls, house fronts turned into shops and markets in the gutter. People were once again allowed to sell their own produce and most people, particularly the older ones who remembered what it was like before the revolution, liked the changes and being less repressed. You would not dare call it capitalism, but it was no longer bad to be rich. A new class of people was emerging, but inflation was causing problems. Inequalities between rich and poor were increasing – prices rose all the time, yet wages remained the same, so how did the poor pay for their rice?

Goods were pushed or pulled over the cobbled streets in wooden hand carts, or pedalled about in the utility pan of a three-wheeled bicycle, or borne by coolies, some naked from the waist up, who strained under terrific loads suspended from bamboo poles on their shoulders. A few years ago this part of the old Chinese city had been highly dangerous for Europeans and it would have cost me my life to enter it. Even now you could still get lost there.

Next day I decided to do a boat tour on the river. According to my book, the tour left from 'a little north' of the Peace Hotel. A little north my foot! It was a fast twenty-minute walk down the Bund. That book has a lot to answer for. The times the tour took varied, depending on who gave me the information. The same boat was said to take two hours, three hours or three and a half hours. The trip in fact took four hours and was a sixty-kilometre round trip up the Huangpu River to where it met the Yangtze. The ship was comfortable, although foreigners paid much more than the Chinese price. In return for this extortion we were seated in the prow in lounge chairs.

The blurb said that we would go where 'one magnificent panorama expanded after another' but we only went down the river I had already come up in the *Hai Sing*. After leaving the magnificence of the Bund, one dreary building after another lined the shore and one rusty ship after another was tied on the muddy water. Even the Bund was partly obscured by smog. We passed the *Hai Sing*. I gave her a wave. Then it rained, preventing me from going out on deck for a lung full of pollution. But any ride on a ship pleases a ship lover. The minute I came aboard I was given tea in a lidded blue and white mug. It was the same green tea that all Chinese drink from large glass jars with a screw-top lid. The first time I saw one of these jars, half-full of clear yellow fluid, standing on the dashboard of a taxi, I thought someone had collected a specimen for the doctor. So imagine my horror when the owner unscrewed the lid and took a drink out of it. Initially I thought it was awful to be using old jars to drink from and wondered why they did not use cups, than I realised what a good idea it was.

The jar was portable – you could drag it around with you all day once the lid was on. The same tea leaves, long worm-like strands of green tea, were left in all day. The jar was topped up now and then with fresh hot water. I was served salted plums with my tea, but I did not realise they had plastic stuck hard to their outsides and once again I ate the wrappings. I got through two before I realised my mistake. I hoped nobody had noticed. I get very hungry travelling and its supposedly typical to be famished again half an hour after eating Chinese meals, but that didn't mean I should eat plastic! Later we were served cup cakes and heavily pre-sugared, lukewarm coffee.

On the return trip a floor show was provided for our diversion. First a young man gave a demonstration of painting the inside of a snuff bottle. I think we were expected to buy one. No one did, and this act went out with a fizzle. The Chinese have funny ideas about what westerners expect or like. Then we were entertained by a magician: a middle-aged man with a middle-aged female assistant, probably his unpaid wife. He was dressed like a 1940s Chicago gangster in a spiv's loud checked jacket and two-toned brown and white shoes, and was heavily Brylcreamed. He looked as though he got his idea of the way westerners dress from watching old movies. But he did some clever tricks, such as cutting off an arm – not his own – inside an Oriental screen with a mini guillotine, and chewing up and swallowing a pile of razor blades. Now, that *is* hungry!

I also visited the temple of the Jade Buddha, which was a little way from the centre of Shanghai. This active temple, built between 1911 and 1918, had seventy resident monks. Its claim to fame was its two priceless white jade statues of the Buddha, which were brought over from Burma in 1882. The larger one, weighing one thousand kilograms and encrusted with jewels, was in the seated position of enlightenment. The smaller one reclined gracefully on a polished wooden bed and three other gold-plated statues kept them company. The temple also housed seven thousand books of Buddhist scriptures which were two hundred years old.

One night I shared my hotel room with a Swiss girl and the next I had three very young, sweet, and clean Japanese students – they spent the whole time washing themselves or their clothes. Every day we were given our government issue rations – packets of disposable soap, toothbrush, toothpaste and comb. And they were truly disposable, one use was all you got. The first time you brushed your teeth the tooth brush curled up like a hairy caterpillar and subsequently died. Using the comb was like dragging razor blades through your hair. The teeth fell out one by one as you tugged on it. The soap, just a sliver cosseted in two lots of wrapping was only good for two hand washings. It didn't lather anyway. The tooth-paste varied in each hotel. I found some that tasted like chewing gum (mind you, Chinese chewing gum tastes like toothpaste) and others that tasted very much like petrol.

(Yes, I do know what petrol tastes like. I've done a bit of syphoning.)

On the day that I was to leave the *Pu Jiang*, the room attendant tried her utmost to get rid of me early in the morning. She seemed most anxious for me to go. Ever since the bed episode she had viewed me with dark sus-picion. She thought I was a trouble-maker. But, as my train to Beijing did not leave until four in the afternoon, I hung in there until exit time at twelve noon. I did not want to be turfed out to walk the streets till then.

9 Beijing express

As I got out of the taxi at the Shanghai railway station a pair of enterprising old ladies appeared with a wooden hand cart and lumped my baggage inside for a small contribution to their retirement fund. The station building was a splendid old pile, as crowded as could be outside but, as entry was strictly policed, was not too busy inside – one of the few places in China that wasn't. Across the massive main hall and through wooden framed swinging glass doors the train stood waiting on the platform.

My first-class, whoops! I mean soft-class – there were no classes in China, only euphemisms for them – compartment was next to the conductor's hidey hole. I wondered if this was the one they had the spy hole in, or if I was being isolated to prevent me contaminating the other passengers. Through the window I watched a large group of military personnel farewelling a person of obviously elevated status. There was much shaking of hands and exchanges of greetings and, as the train began to pull out, the exalted one climbed aboard.

Instantly the line of soldiers along the platform sprang to attention and stood stiffly, saluting as the train inched past. Their faces were very close to mine. The first passed, then the second and when the third one, looking straight ahead, deadpan serious, caught my eye, I gave in to an uncontrollable urge and winked at him. His face twitched and started to crack up and I saw, by gosh, that he was going to laugh. I felt awful then in case he got into trouble, but the temptation was too great.

Leaving Shanghai we passed through the same boring clutter that surrounds any city train station. Soon we were out in the country. I was pleasantly surprised at how much green there was. My first impressions of China had been that it was all a dreary brown and covered with a film of smog. But now I saw cultivation. Every inch and conceivable piece of ground was used, only for edible items, of course – there were cabbages galore. I delighted in the rows of different shades of greens. The varying heights of the crops made interesting patterns. The vegetables were down low, the maize or barley was waist high, and then clumps of tall bamboo and vines stood tall.

Before long thin, lofty pine trees appeared along the edges of the railway line and a little further on square rice paddies started. There was no open or uninhabited land. The countryside was dotted with barefoot men and women working their small plots of ground. They hoed the soil and dipped water from ponds to pour on their vegetables from wooden buckets that swung from yokes on their shoulders.

Feeding everyone is a perennial problem in China. They just have too many people, despite the world's most severe family planning program and restrictions on internal migration. The government is trying to keep them down on the farm. And food problems are exacerbated by floods and droughts. But since new policies have allowed the majority of peasants to sell the surplus from their private gardens and cottage industries, rural profits have slowly risen.

For a while the road ran alongside the train line and I could see that the traffic on it, apart from the odd bus or elderly truck, was mostly propelled by pedal power. I saw a bridge, a graceful curve of stone, that was just like the ones painted on the blue and white willow pattern plates often seen on kitchen dressers. We passed through a few well-kept stations and many villages. The houses of one big village had pagoda-like roof corners lifting skywards, but all the other housing I saw was strictly utilitarian.

I was alone in my train compartment. It was a luxurious den where lace and velvet had been used everywhere possible. Royal-blue velvet curtains overlaid white lace curtains, the bunks had pleated royal-blue velvet edged covers, velvet pads with hand-embroidered lace covers adorned the backs of the seats, and the table had a white lace cover. There were frilly pillow cases, embroidered blankets and sheets, and even a hand-crocheted royal-blue coathanger. Even Queen Victoria would have approved! There was space to put your luggage under the seats, a heater, air-conditioning, lights, a loud speaker, and even a 'no smoking' sign. Unfortunately the heater only worked when the government allowed it, only half the lights worked, the Chinese smoked when and where they liked, and the loud speaker could not be turned off.

The attendant, a severe young woman, brought me a pair of plastic slippers (male orientated and miles too big) and toothbrush and toothpaste. I was also given a gift – a folding plastic coathanger, which may have come in handy if I had ever worked out how to unfold it and get something to stay on its extremely slippery sides. Presents seem to be *de rigeur* in China. I received a present when I took the river cruise in Shanghai – a badge, and, of all things, a cotton tea tray cover, just what you need when travelling.

It was sometimes hard to fathom how the Chinese perceive us westerners. They have the world's longest running civilisation. Their recorded history goes back four thousand years and for the last two thousand they firmly believed that they were the only civilised country on earth and that no other country had anything of value to offer them. Until the late 1970s tourists were almost unknown in China, which had been virtually closed to travellers for thirty years. Independent travel has only recently been permitted, and I can vouch for the fact that it is still difficult.

After a while the conductor brought someone to share my compartment, a venerable and charming Chinese gentleman with a benign and serene countenance. He looked like the pictures of wise old Mandarins of the past, except that he wore a blue Mao suit. A female relative settled him in – the Chinese are rarely alone. I think he had been moved so that he could have a lower berth. The Chinese don't like top bunks, and no wonder. You needed the agility of a monkey to get up to the top bunks. No ladder was provided for access, just a tiny foothold on the wall. From this point you had to swing upwards on a wing and a prayer and hope you made it. This was dicey at any time but in my stockinged feet it was dangerous. But I was to learn, as I progressed to more crowded trains, that at least up top no one came and sat on you.

The old gentleman was extremely gracious. We bowed to each other and said, 'Ni hao.' Hello. That exhausted my Chinese conversation. The Mandarin proceeded to arrange himself. On the table he set out his accoutrements of travel: an enormous lidded enamel tin mug, which would have done any shearer proud and would have held at least three cups of tea, an enamel bowl, and a couple of bags of food (he did not eat in the dining car). He covered his bowl with a square of cloth, positioned the pillow he had brought with him and was then ready for his tea. I helped him pour it. The massive thermos was so heavy it was difficult to manage in a moving train.

The conductor collected an order for my evening meal and extracted a small sum of money from me. I had no idea what I had ordered, but I am an optimist. At feeding time she returned and led me to the dining car. This was, like the compartments, decorated in blue and white – pale-blue velvet curtains, dark blue slip covers on the chairs, white lace curtains, white tablecloths and frilly bits and pieces everywhere. An abundance of smartly togged staff loitered everywhere. The waiters and kitchen staff had their hair covered by old-fashioned head dresses, like veils.

I had already noticed the surplus of staff in China, many of whom were there in a decorative capacity to impress the patrons. Two girls in stylish uniforms, for example, would often be stationed on either side of the entrance door at smart hotels. They just stood, the doorman opened the door. These living dolls were even positioned at the doors of supermarkets. At first I wondered if they were watching for shop-lifters, but guards also stood by the check out and at the entrance to the aisles. Sometimes these human ornaments were stuck up on a pedestal, a live statue. The first time I saw this statue impersonation was at the entrance to the Shanghai railway station, where a policeman posed up on a plinth. He looked so lifelike that I stared and stared until with a jolt I realised that he was staring back. He was real! Just as well I hadn't given in to my initial urge to poke him.

At dinner on the train I was astounded at the amount of food I saw wasted. And this was the land of Pearl

Buck's famous book, *The Good Earth*, which gives harrowing accounts of millions of Chinese people dying of starvation and thousands surviving only by eating soup made out of earth, grass and anything else they could find. Yet here were Chinese people throwing out food by the cart load. And it did go in the bins. I saw them, brimming over, and not a pig in sight to benefit. Sharing my table was a couple who had twelve plates of food, as well as bowls of rice and soup, put in front of them. Across the aisle, one man eating alone had six plates of food, and he ate from only two. The untouched food was taken away in the same state as it arrived.

I saw bottles of beer on some tables and decided that it was a good idea. I toddled down the aisle and bought a room temperature beer from a man seated at a tiny counter at the other end of the dining car. Why this was necessary beats me; the waiters could easily have done it. But I noticed that the person selling usually did not handle the money; you had to go and pay someone else. Once the food was on the tables the beer seller disappeared quickly and the diner's chance was over. They were not encouraging dipsomaniacs on this train.

The compartment I was in had four bunks but was only occupied by the Mandarin and me all the way to Beijing. When it was time to get up in the morning he considerately went away for quite a while so that I could get out of bed without embarrassment. This was handy as, although I had gone to bed almost fully clothed, I had shed my clothes during the night as it got warmer. I opened one eye just on dawn and saw that he was gone. Probably already doing his tai-chi in the corridor, I thought, and went back to sleep. He had been sound asleep by seven o'clock the night before; no wonder they get up with the birds.

The carriage had a washroom with two hand basins where I performed my ablutions, pedalling on the foot pedal to pump up the water. I desisted from this practice in trains after later seeing a male guard using the basin in the washroom as a urinal when the loo was in use. There were two toilets, a western pedestal and an Asian hole-in-the-floor squat job, and both opened directly onto the ground. The pedestal toilet smelled awful. The squat hole was slightly cleaner, but by the end of the journey both of them stank.

I never saw a public toilet in China that was not disgusting. I had been warned about the foul Chinese train loos by other travellers and had read the bitter complaint that all public toilets were 'vile at forty feet'. This train was the tourist show case – the toilets got much worse as I progressed to lesser trains.

I was always amazed to see neat Chinese girls stepping daintily out of a reeking toilet with no sign of displeasure on their faces. If this was soft class, the loos in hard class did not bear thinking about. There, the carriage floor was a bad enough sight, covered with spit, tea dregs, peels, shells and the puddles the babies made via their split pants.

Morning found us nearing Beijing, about eighteen hours and fifteen hundred miles from Shanghai. It was pretty country, with large expanses of fields, edged by poplar trees, in which sunflowers grew in brilliant profusion along with corn and vegies. Now there were fewer houses and people, and some sheep, cows, horses and a black pig or two. Mule and horse carts ambled along a little path that ran next to the train.

I looked in vain for wildlife. It seemed true that the only wildlife you see in China is on the dinner plate – snake, monkey, dog, cat, ant eater, raccoon, bear, giant salamander. In the north-east and Hunan province there are said to be bears, tigers, moose, reindeer and deer. But for how long? Many Chinese believe that animals do not feel pain and that the animals are on earth to be used, abused and eaten by man. Restaurant windows exhibited tanks of live fish that waited to be selected for someone's meal and sometimes the fish would only be given an inch of water in which they gasped and flopped and barely stayed alive.

Beijing, China's capital, covers sixteen thousand square kilometres and houses a population of ten million. Peking Man settled down near present day Beijing about 500,000 years ago.

The earliest records of settlement date from 1000 BC when it was a frontier trading town. By 1215 AD, when Ghenghis Khan's Mongol hordes conquered the city, it had become the capital of the Yan Kingdom. Khubla Khan, Ghenghis Khan's grandson, ruled most of Asia by 1279. He established the Yuan dynasty in China and built a city called Dadu on the site of present day Beijing. Marco Polo and other western travellers who visited China around this time brought back tales of its wonders to Europe. Khubla Khan lived to be eighty and was a generous and religiously tolerant ruler. After he died, decline set in and China was invaded by the Manchu, who founded the Ming dynasty in 1368.

The first thing I had to do in Beijing was find Monkey Business and give them my Mongolian visa application. I gave their address, written in Chinese, to the taxi driver, but it still took some finding. We ended up alongside the canal. The minute we left the main road we were in deep rutted lanes and waterlogged unpaved tracks. The driver stopped beside a man flying a kite, who gave us directions. Monkey Business is run by a group of very 'allo allo' Frenchmen. The staff directed me to a hotel, not cheap by Asian standards, but very reasonable for

Beijing: twenty-nine dollars. I was adjusting to Chinese prices. Chinese pay a dollar for a hotel, we pay thirty.

The Jing Hua Hotel, like all Chinese hotels, insisted on up front payment. You didn't get a foot inside their hallowed halls without laying down your cash, plus a two hundred *yuan* deposit for the key – more than the price of the room – in case you took off with the towels. I needed to change some money in order to pay. Ever mindful that carrying a lot of cash is not a good idea, you never seem to change enough money when travelling.

The Jing Hua did not change money, but they directed me to another hotel that did. 'You can't miss it. It's just round the corner.'

Oh terrible phrase! It took two and a half hours, lots of walking and several sets of directions.

One difficulty in finding hotels in China is that not all of them look like hotels from the outside, nor quite a few from the inside too, and not all have signs announcing their business – at least not ones that I could understand.

Building cranes obtruded on the skyline wherever I looked. It seemed that most of Beijing was new, but the Beijing buildings were usually unattractive, identical square blocks. Much of the housing seemed to be ready-made slums.

I found it rather sad that in Beijing, the history of which goes back three thousand years, there were only a few structures that were old, pleasing, or of Chinese appearance. In the back streets I occasionally glimpsed a traditional compound surrounded by a high wall with a circular moon gate, behind which stood a carved screen. (The screen foiled any bad fairies trying to get in by mucking up their radar.) But I liked the wide boulevards, well kept and clean, that had enormous bicycle lanes to keep cyclists separated from the other traffic.

Although motorists still drove in a haphazard way,

the traffic was not heavy and it was not instant death to mingle in it the way it was in Shanghai. Unless you meandered into it looking in the wrong direction the way I did.

I eventually found the hotel that changed money, but the young lady in reception conveyed to me, using sign language, that the person who performed this function was absent. She pointed to one o'clock on my watch. An English sign on the desk was encouraging: 'Guest the highest, service the first, we were keenly expecting you and your friends.' The foyer was festooned with Christmas decorations – in September – and was blessed with the scent of pink Lorraine Lee roses that lined the street in row after row outside. I decided to lunch while I waited and, wandering around in the maze of corridors, visited all the lavatories, including the gents, while trying to find the restaurant. Once there I showed off my prowess with chopsticks to the audience I had by now become accustomed to.

Returning to the front desk I found two new receptionists installed there. They answered my eager enquiry about money with the news that the change person would not be back until two. I sat down in front of the counter to read my guidebook. I wanted them to remember I was there. At half-past one a man appeared. No one gave any indication that this was the man I so anxiously awaited. I think they would have let me sit there all day. After a while, fearful that he might disappear for good, I approached this gentleman with the supposition that he might be the Money Fairy and he admitted, under interrogation, that he was indeed the one with the keys to the cash box.

The Jing Hua Hotel had none of the colonial elegance of the one in Shanghai. Here we were reduced to tacky plastic chandeliers. My room was on the sixth floor. There was a lift, but it had a very casual attendant. You summoned her by phone and, if it was your lucky day, she would come to get you. If not, you walked up or down six flights of stairs. The Jing Hua was riddled with cockroaches, but it had most facilities, some of which even worked. A sign in my room boasted that it had an 'alarming system'. I believed it. The bathroom floor was always awash with water – the shower ran straight onto the floor and water escaped into the bedroom, wetting the filthy carpet. In the shower, as there was no rose, you got a deadly assault with a hard jet of water. The toilets were perpetually blocked, the air-conditioner only worked now and then and, depending on wind direction, the most horrible stench wafted in off the river running alongside the hotel. This sad stream was used as a rubbish dump and was an open sewer. All the local toilets emptied into it.

Only one of the hotel desk staff knew a few words of English, but one of the rooms on the first floor contained a small independent tour operator called Mr Fu. He spoke English fluently and was always ready to help. He arranged for me to join a bus trip to the Great Wall on the following day. Mr Fu also ran a back-packers' dormitory on the first floor. With double racks of bunks crammed the entire length of a long narrow room, it looked like a cell block in a frightful primitive prison.

I gave Mr Fu the cigarettes I won on the ship. They were called Double Happiness, and I hoped that didn't mean they were 'funny' ciggies.

That evening I sampled the fare at the local restaurant, a prefab hut that had been carelessly dumped on the footpath next to the hotel entrance. You ate either inside or outside at tables and chairs on the footpath, depending on which way the wind was blowing off the river. It sounds atrocious, but it was quite charming.

Nearby was another temporary structure, a mixture of shed and barn. The enigmatic legend 'Bar and Kok', was blazoned across its front. I worked out that Kok meant karaoke, which was now all the rage in China. The sweet, young giggling waiters in the restaurant were eager to help me with the menu, which had attempted English subtitles and thoroughly fractured them. I ordered a chicken dish, which was great, and a plate of what was said to be 'hollow fried vegetables'. They were certainly hollow, with bits of leaves attached, but I have no idea what that mound of green stuff I munched through was. It tasted rather like horse food. I tried to order beer, but it only came in huge brown bottles, and I only wanted a little. I pointed to the next item on the list, which was written as 'wine'. My helpers re-translated the English for me and pronounced it to be tea. It cost thirty cents, so I figured it couldn't be anything exotic. I pointed to the Chinese alongside the English and the waitress repeated 'tea'. I agreed to try that.

A small five ounce bottle of something that certainly wasn't tea arrived. Thinking it was wine, I poured the clear fluid into the bulky tumbler provided. Funny looking wine, I thought, but maybe that's Chinese wine. I swallowed a mouthful and nearly exploded – my hair stood straight up on end. It was spirit. And I mean spirit, as in rocket fuel! I gathered, from the way it was served, that I was meant to drink the lot at one sitting, but I knew there was no way I would ever get up from the table if I did. So, not wanting to be beaten entirely, I poured all except half an inch back into the bottle, and topped up my ration with some of the dreadful local fizzy lolly water. I drank the 'wine' with my meal. By the time I reached the bottom of the glass my eyesight was going, and I had a buzzing in my ears and a constriction in my chest. It would have been impossible for me to drink even one more of those shots. I'd have been dead if I'd drunk the bottle. I left unsteadily, clutching the bottle, determined to have the contents analysed. I discovered later it was Chinese whisky.

My next episode in that restaurant I think of as the Night of the Fish – Jaws on a Plate. I ordered sweet and sour fish, which took an inordinate time to appear. Looking at the menu again I noticed the price for the first time. Oh, no! Not a whole fish, I prayed. It was. The little waitress finally appeared, tottering under the weight of a massive platter and peering over a whale of a fish that hung, head and tail, off both edges.

In the mornings I availed myself of the breakfast served in the hotel dining room. The room had a concrete floor and the ambience of a milking shed and was hidden behind a deceptively swank entrance that was screened by a massive piece of glass luridly painted with tropical fish. After you had passed the screen, you moved along a grotty passage piled high on both sides with wicker baskets brimming over with dirty laundry, until you came to the dining room (which must moonlight as the laundry). At the food issuing counter I was given a plastic, compartmented tray that held a pile of cold red salted and pickled cabbage (an acquired taste); a hot steamed dumpling filled with spiced, minced meat; another dumpling filled with mucky stuff that looked like chocolate, but tasted frightful; and yet another dumpling without filling which was like trying to swallow cotton wool; a bowl of positively horrible gruel porridge; two slices of dry bread; sundry unidentifiable objects; and one egg fried in oil. One morning there was fried lettuce, which I liked. The cooking of the eggs was accomplished *in situ*, on a burner sitting on a steel plate on the counter. No eating irons were in sight. Have you ever tried to eat a runny fried egg with chopsticks?

Believe me, you don't want to. There was a splodge of something on my tray that looked like tomato sauce, so I piled it on my egg. It was plum jam. I ate it. I also ate my Chinese neighbour's dumpling and her plum jam that she kindly offered me.

As a special dispensation, my 'big-nosed' – the Chinese refer to westerners as *dabidze* or big nose – western face was offered coffee. It came heavily milked and sugared in a medium sized soup bowl. I took this back and, to avoid mistakes and stay the cook's hand from the sugar pot, I stood by him while he prepared the second one. He was incredulous that anyone would refuse sugar. The next morning he showed me proudly that he remembered how I liked my coffee. But he did not measure it with a spoon, he just tipped it from the container into my bowl. I must have got a quarter of a jar. It was so strong it curled my teeth and I was hyperactive until lunch time.

One morning I was joined by a Dutchman. He said, 'Look at this place. The floor is filthy.' His Chinese wife was embarrassed. I said nothing. It was true, but I wasn't eating off the floor, and the breakfasts were good. I ate hers too.

It is said that the Chinese eat anything. After seeing chicken-foot stew, cow-tendon soup and hundred-year eggs, I accepted that they look at things differently from westerners. They save urine from public toilets and use the enzymes in it to make medicine. They use dried lizards to treat high blood pressure, and donkey umbilical cords and bird beaks for other ailments.

I took an active dislike to Beijing cockroaches. I am not mad about cockroaches at any time, but I can tolerate them if they behave in the decently furtive manner to which I am accustomed. But when they boldly venture forth in full daylight and cheekily walk over the bed while you are still in it, or take a stroll across the television screen while you are watching it, or tramp through to the bathroom in front of you, then I think they have exceeded their authority and should be told their place. When I discovered that I had unwittingly brought one from Hong Kong as an illegal immigrant in my bag, I went out and bought some insect spray.

The loo in my room had a basket alongside it for used toilet paper. This was a common sight in China, indicating that the condition of the plumbing would not stand the added stress of paper. Every morning the room attendant emptied the basket and dished out the daily ration of lavatory paper, which was treated like gold. You got half a roll a day. If you needed more you had to go begging for it, clutching the empty cardboard holder to prove it had been used and that you were not hoarding this treasure.

10 Donkey business

I watched an old lady do her morning shadow boxing exercises on the pavement outside the hotel as I sat in the bus waiting to go to the Wall. After forty minutes the other tourists straggled up. A tall, thin young German back-packer with a scraggy beard and granny glasses sat next to me. Two young Chinese men were our escorts – one to drive, and the other to watch him drive. Neither spoke a word of anything but Chinese, the tourists had most languages except Chinese, but we got by. The driver opened a big, steaming jar of tea, stood it on the dashboard, put his head down and slurped. His mate took off his shoes, put his sock-covered feet up on the windscreen and promptly went to sleep for an hour. I wished he had continued this occupation, because when he woke up he started shouting and didn't stop. Almost all the Chinese talk very loudly, perhaps in the need to be heard above the mob.

Simatai, the site at the Wall we were heading for, was a three-hour ride away, one hundred and twenty kilometres to the north-east. We crossed downtown Beijing – big, boring blocks of concrete, but further out were public parks with trees and huge tracts of roses. The blooms were smaller than in Australia, but they smelled fantastic. After an hour we left the city and drove through the countryside on an expressway divided by a median strip on which huge poplar trees grew ten abreast.

Poplars also lined the sides of the road, lovely graceful trees standing tall and straight like a row of soldiers. The lower part of their trunks had been painted white to serve as road markers. I saw council workers pedalling their equipment about in bicycle carts. One of these bicycle brigades composed a battalion of little ladies, who were busy wielding big whitewash brushes, sloshing paint on the trees. (And a fair bit of the road into the bargain.) As well as the roadside poplars there were fir and spruce trees and numerous types of pine: some similar to Australian native pines and others with massive branches like Norfolk Island pines. When we were well in the country, trees stood ten deep either side of the road. Behind the trees were fields of corn, fat white geese paddling on creeks and ponds, and small flocks of goats. Every piece of precious livestock had an attendant. As we climbed higher towards the mountains, apple and pear orchards began to appear.

Occasionally we passed through a village with small houses, not old, but built close together with their backs to the road or railway line, giving the impression that the villages were walled.

We stopped at one provincial town – I can't say small as no place in China is small – where we were shepherded into a local shop for provisions. It probably belonged to a relative of the driver. The shop was an immense barn of a place, with terrazzo floors and big aisles between old-fashioned glass-topped counters. Large squads of staff stood about doing nothing in this deserted void. One extensive brown wooden counter had four girls spaced along behind it, decorative but useless: there were no customers. As I walked along one of the five metre wide aisles, an assistant took a swig from her tea jar, siphoned up some tea leaves and spat them, with a vast mouthful of tea, straight onto the floor right in front of my feet. Looking around I saw evidence of previous squirts all over the floor. I was flabbergasted. It must be common practice.

The shop goods consisted of truckloads of unwrapped buns and utilitarian biscuits sitting under the glass of the counters or on the open shelves behind. There was a limited variety of other edible merchandise spread out over a sizeable area to make it appear more. I bought a bun that was extremely cheap at two cents, but tasteless, and some bananas, which were much the same price as in Australia.

Then, there it was, the Great Wall, the only man-made thing on earth visible from space. Six thousand, three hundred and fifty kilometres long, it undulated across the tops of the mountains like an elongated Chinese dragon. The Wall crosses five provinces and two autonomous regions, from the sea of the east coast to the sands of the Gobi desert, at times at a height of one thousand metres above sea level. Commenced by the first Chin emperor over two thousand years ago, the wall was built to protect China from the Hun and other Northern wild men considered anti-social at the time. It supposedly became the world's biggest graveyard, as many of the slaves, convicts and political prisoners who died building it – said to have been one man for every metre – were buried where they fell. Communist literature refers to it as 'a monument to vainglorious feudal tyranny'. They were right for once. On top of the wall, at a height of 7.8 metres, ten soldiers could stride side by side between the watch towers positioned every few hundred yards.

The Simatai portion was built in the Ming dynasty, when the wall marched in grandeur across the entire Chinese frontier and emerged from the mountains to run down to the sea. There were several places where the wall could be climbed. Badaling, where most of the tourists were taken, was close to Beijing and the easiest; there were even cable cars to whisk you up. But you can't move there for the hordes of people – the Chinese are keen tourists too, and there are a lot of them. The wall at Simatai had only just become accessible and as it was a long way from Beijing there were few visitors. Here the wall was in its least touristy state and you could find a space to contemplate its majesty in peace. Nineteen kilometres of the wall, containing one hundred and thirty-five watch towers and walls within walls, designed for fighting off any marauders who managed to get that far, remained in an original, if slightly crumbling, state. I was soon to discover that the climb here was not only difficult, it could also be extremely dangerous. There were no hand rails and at times there were barely footholds on the seventy degree inclines. This jaunt was not for anyone with vertigo.

There were, thank goodness, no shops or other tourist trappings. Only a few enterprising vendors had discovered Simatai, and had taken up strategic positions to offer wares: mostly the super-fresh juicy apples and pears from the trees that grew all around, and the ubiquitous postcards.

We left the bus in a parking area high in the mountains and set off on the lengthy walk to the point where the steep climb up to the wall began. Even from that distance I could see how spectacular it was, perched along the sharp mountain spines, the wall curving to their shape as though it was part of them.

Near the start of the path I passed a young fellow offering an alternative means of making the ascent – a donkey! I had only gone a short way along the track when I rounded a bend and, looking up, saw what was in store. I had not realised the extent of the climb. The path stretched upwards, endlessly twisting round and round before it reached the mountain top where the steps to the wall started. The sight of people dotted along the path, appearing smaller and smaller, stopped me in my tracks. It looked as though they were ascending to the biblical heavens.

As I stood there gaping, an American woman passed me on her way back. She said, 'It's too hard. I have given up.' I turned back and eyed the donkey, which suddenly appeared as a very attractive proposition for an anti-exercise couch potato. I negotiated a price to ride him one way. I figured even I could walk back down. The vendors clapped and cheered. I soon found out why. I climbed aboard the donkey and put my feet in the stirrups, an act that didn't please the reluctant donkey. He kicked, shied and tried to bite me. Wise donkey, he knew what was in store for him! I would have kicked and tried to bite too.

My mount needed considerable encouragement. As we finally got into gear, I put up my pink parasol with a pop, frightening the donkey so much that we nearly got to the top at full gallop. After settling down again, we climbed the first incline with the donkey's guardian leading the way. Then we came to the steps. I looked at them appalled. 'Crikey,' I said, 'I can't go up there on a donkey. He'll never make it with me on his back.' Some of the steps were almost perpendicular and only a couple of inches wide.

The guide said something in Chinese that I presumed was 'Hup! Hup! Hup!' He did not beat the donkey or treat him cruelly, which pleased me. On this command the donkey certainly went Hup, literally jumping up the first step. I clamped my legs and clung desperately, still holding the parasol aloft with one hand. Maybe, I thought wildly, it would act as a parachute when we went over the deteriorated rock edge, only inches away, and plummeted to the bottom.

It got worse. The path now rose straight up, almost vertical, with nothing to stop you going over the side. I wanted out. But not the quick way, straight down! The donkey slipped, stumbled, and slithered every now and then as it scooted up steps that became steeper and steeper. I fastened a dead lock on the pommel and leaned forward to ease the weight on the donkey's back. I felt terrible making the donkey do this, but he reached the top without even panting. I can't say the same for me.

After the donkey had negotiated a particularly nasty set of steps, I gave him a congratulatory pat on the neck. He took this as a command and promptly lunged forward, almost breaking into a canter that bounced my heart right into my mouth. Now and then we passed tourists sweating and toiling up or down the path in the sun and I felt a bit of a fool perched on my faithful mount, but not enough to dismount. When we reached the top the guide turned to me with a big grin and said, 'Gentleman go up donkey' – I hope he did not mean that – 'Lady never.' Now he tells me! With any luck the gentlemen were all ex-rodeo riders. You needed to be. I may have been the first but it was definitely the last for me. My knees shook for some time after. There was no way I would have ridden back down.

Even though the descent was easier, you still had to be very careful. The precipitous steps were so narrow at times that you could only put your foot sideways on them. They had been polished smooth by thousands of climbers over the centuries and were dangerously slippery. As I carefully picked my way down, rocks slid from under my feet and dropped over the ragged edge bouncing down the sheer precipice.

The end of the path where I parted company with the donkey was still nowhere near the wall – a thousand or more steps had to be climbed to reach it. On I crawled, skywards, only resting now and then. A small girl attached herself to me and refused to go away until I bought some of her postcards. She climbed several hundred steps with me before she produced them and several hundred more before I, in desperation, finally bought the bloody things. Then off she skipped.

At the top the view was spectacular. And the Great Wall was stupendous, not so much for its size and length, but for the incredibly difficult terrain it traversed as it snaked along. I looked down into the sloping sides of wooded mountains and a lake in the middle of the valley way below where people in boats looked like insects. It was grand to sit on the wall and commune with nature and breathe the clean air. The sky was blue and I could see for miles.

Down at ground level once more I walked past my donkey and, overcome with gratitude, bought an apple and fed it to him. He loved it!

After several attempts to get in the wrong bus – they all looked the same and I couldn't ask for help – I located our driver in a refreshment stop close by and sat down near him (did I mention that he was young and handsome?) to wait for the others.

I was entertained by the sight and sound of men spitting on the floor, before, during and after meals. They spit in waste baskets, around trees and on any floor at all, even carpets.

I was directed to the toilet by the waitress, but took a wrong turn. I realised after that I had used one in a private compound – a commune of attached dwellings built around an open square – belonging to local workers. As I passed through the yard I looked through the glass-less windows of the houses. The interiors were neat but bare. The toilets around the back had no doors, just a waist high concrete screen in front of them, and were the dire squat jobs. The one I used could possibly have been the gents. I couldn't read the sign on it, so I stuck my umbrella on top of a post outside, like a totem, to warn others of my occupancy.

Back in the cafe I watched a Frenchman desperately asking the staff for the same convenience. They stead-fastly ignored him, refusing to understand. Perhaps his grotty appearance had something to do with it. Taking pity on him I conducted him to the place I had been, and even gave him some toilet paper.

We returned to Beijing at dusk, having spent four hours at the wall and six hours getting there and back.

Early next morning I went downtown to the Friend-ship Store and bought a map, which was a complicated procedure. First I gave the map to an assistant with a promise to buy it, then I took my money to a cashier, returned to the assistant with a stamped receipt in tripli-cate, and was given the goods. In the cosmetic department I was amused by a face cream said to be 'for senile fleck removing' on one side and 'flack speckle removal' on the other. There was also other stuff that promised to 'degrade' (debride) you. Terrific!

A pleasant walk along a broad, tree lined boulevard, where sentries stood on the alert at the gates of pala-tial, but unattractive, square buildings, brought me to the silk market. Behind the sentries and the walls were gardens sporting an abundance of trees and roses. There were even flowers in pots on the footpath; possibly put there to impress the visitors to the Women's Conference.

This downtown area of Beijing was what official visitors were shown, not the back streets. A banner in the main drag said, 'Welcome and Good Luck to the Women's Conference.' Another said, 'Rights for Women.' I thought that rights were not something the government cared much about. What about rights for oppressed minorities like Tibet and Inner Mongolia, who had been forced under China's domination?

I was told that during the conference the factories were closed, beggars were shunted out of town, and people were forbidden to drive into the city. An entire suburb of apartment buildings was commandeered to house the four thousand delegates. When asked where the usual residents were, the visitors were told that they had all gone on holiday. No one believed it. While the Olympic Games committee was inspecting Beijing, the same steps to improve China's image had been taken. The city had been cleaned up, spitting had been stopped, and heating and hot water was turned off – Chinese officials did not want the pollution from coal burning to be seen.

The silk market consisted of row after row of small stalls that took me two hours to get around at a fast trot. Preparing for the cold of Mongolia, I invested in a down-filled coat – a monstrosity of mammoth proportions, thick long underpants and woolly socks.

Near my hotel I saw a crowd gathered in the street and found they were reading newspapers and notices, including photos of criminals and executions, that hung on a wall in wooden frames. Capital punishment was the arbitrary sentence for murder, arson, rape, swindling and theft. Every now and then a big event was staged in a stadium where a large number of condemned felons were publicly executed to the cheers and applause of the packed audience. Between 1983 and 1986 one hundred thousand executions were carried out. The deed was done by applying a bullet to the back of the neck. The criminals' photos were displayed in their home town on the railway or post office wall. A red mark was put on the pictures of those who had been executed, sometimes with a photo of the execution. Someone caught red-handed could be executed on the spot. It was a drastic and final solution to crime. The Chinese theory is that 'you kill a chicken to scare the monkeys'.

I was leaving at six the next morning, so I tried to get my key money refunded that night. This request was refused because the room attendant needed to check the room after I had left it to see that I hadn't pinched, broken or burned holes in any of their precious cargo. Posted on the wall of my room was a list of fines for offences ranging from chipping the tiles to swiping the sheets. The management did not trust a soul. Uniformed guards were stationed at strategic spots around the ground floor. The tins of soft drink and bottles of juice displayed in the hotel foyer's shop were empty. The real ones were under lock and key. Nice type of guest they must get here.

I had just gone to sleep when the phone by the bed woke me with a start. I think it was an obscene phone call, but unfortunately I couldn't understand a word. Just my luck.

Monkey Business had arranged to collect Mongolia-bound travellers from the foyer of the Jing Hua and, at the appointed hour, I was perched on a bench waiting. After half an hour or so, a mini bus arrived with our keepers – two bleary-eyed Frenchmen whose job it was to deliver us to the station and escort us onto the train.

It was not quite day when we set off and it had been

raining. In the misty grey half-light I saw that people were already out and about on the wet pavements doing tai-chi and exercises or selling goods from small stalls. The outside of the station, a huge building with a tower each end sporting pagoda roofs, was crowded with buses and people. We made our way over smooth tiled floors and passed through a heavily guarded turnstile onto the platform. It was no real hassle to board the train, the Trans Siberian Express, as I had been warned it usually was. I think Monkey may have told me it would be to frighten me from going alone. I discovered that the crush usually only applies to hard seat travel. We were travelling in the equivalent of a second class sleeper. Our group got acquainted on the platform. There were thirteen of us. All except one American woman and I were going on to Russia after a ten-day stop-over in Outer Mongolia.

At half past seven the train moved slowly out of the station heading north-west. When the sun came up it was pleasantly warm and soon we were passing through the mountains. At Badaling I saw the Great Wall again, crossing the mountain peaks and continuing as far as I could see into the distance. Slightly shrouded in morning mist, it looked ethereal and even more like a great stone serpent. The train went through many tunnels to pass through to the other side of this range of high mountains. Having reached the highest point we were shunted onto a switch rail. On the downhill journey, the engine was put in front as it no longer needed to push from behind.

Soon we were travelling through open country, where a blue-grey range of mountains on the horizon formed a backdrop for the view from the train. In the foreground neat plots of green vegetables and fields of ripe corn and sunflowers made pretty patchwork squares. We passed lines of graceful emerald willows bordering canals and paddocks of pink roses, and houses whose roofs were covered with orange corn cobs drying in the sun. Donkey power seemed to be the main method of pulling carts and moving burdens. We passed through several industrial cities where multitudes of ugly chimneys belched black smoke over drab apartment buildings. In some of the villages I saw peasants wearing blue Mao suits. You see less of this form of dress in cities now. Although some conservatives still cling to these uniforms, along with their austerity principles, most people wear bright colours. But fashion has a long way to go.

I wondered at the lack of birds until I read about Chairman Mao's 'Campaign of the Four Pests' – mozzies, flies, rats and birds, particularly sparrows – during which everyone had a quota to kill per day. Highly commendable in the first three instances but pure stupidity in the last.

Now that we travellers were about to leave China we discussed our experiences and summarised our feelings about the country. I decided that, although no one had understood a word I said and it had been difficult to find my way about because few signs were comprehensible, I had not had the hard time I was told to expect. Perhaps it was best to expect the worst. At least in China it was perfectly proper to do many things that were socially unacceptable at home. All those things your mother told you never to do were okay. You could, if you felt so inclined, pick your nose, slurp your food, spit on the floor, push, shove, be rude to strangers and throw your lolly papers in the street.

11 Into the mountains of Mongolia

By afternoon we had sped through the outer Chinese province of Hebei and were clickety clacking our way through Inner Mongolia. Bare hills rose gently behind plains of low grass and fields of barley and wheat, some of which was being harvested by cheerful workers. Armed with scythes, they straightened up among the stook-dotted fields to wave and smile as we passed. Others digging potatoes from large plots on the sloping sides of the train tracks, paused to watch and wave too. Behind them piles of big yellow spuds lay on the freshly dug earth.

Now and then I saw small flocks of sheep or goats, a few cows, or a man ploughing a field with two bullocks or a horse. The villages were large, with ugly, square brick houses, from which children rushed excitedly to wave as the train passed. Copses of birches, the shape of a closed umbrella, flourished along the railway line and around villages and fields. The air was clean and across the intense blue of the sky lolled a few white clouds.

Inner Mongolia is a Chinese autonomous region. This means that the people govern themselves, but in reality they are Chinese ruled, like the Tibetans. Try telling *them* they are autonomous. In the mid-seventeenth century the Manchurians of north-east China invaded southern Mongolia taking advantage of the internal strife among the Mongolian Khans. They made it a vassal state and named it Inner Mongolia. Since then the northern part of the country that managed to remain independent has been referred to as Outer Mongolia.

Primitive man settled in Mongolia 300,000 to 350,000 years ago. By the late third century BC the dominant tribes had united to form a strong nomadic empire. The harsh climate produced a tough people; by the year 1280 they had conquered half the world on horseback! The Mongolians had tenacity. Instead of hibernating during the severe winters, they waited for the rivers to freeze and rode over the ice to continue their campaigns. They went everywhere, at all times, and were afraid of only one thing – lightning. Stand out in the vast open grasslands in a storm and you'll understand why.

Temujin Ghenghis Khan was born about 1162. When he was young his father, the leader of the Kiyat-Borjigins, was poisoned by rival Tatars and subsequently his child-hood and adolescence were times of privation and hostility. In 1206 he was made the Great Khan and given the Mongolian throne and the title Ghenghis Khan, universal ruler, by the people. He founded a strong centralised government that was more democratic than most countries then and many now. Despite his reputation for cruelty and vindictiveness he was fair and magnanimous, and he valued honesty above all else. A brilliant tactician and leader, he won his splendid victories due to discipline, organisation and skill. He is still described as the greatest military genius in history.

Ghenghis Khan died in 1227 after falling from his horse in a campaign, and is possibly buried in the Khenty Mountains. Expeditions are still searching for the tomb of the Great Khan, but the Mongol people object. Recently the newspaper printed a demand that the searching stop – the Mongol people did not want his tomb desecrated, but kept sacrosanct and secret for all time.

It was his grandson, Khubla Khan, who subjugated China and set himself up in Beijing to start the Yuan dynasty. This was the height of glory for the Mongol empire. It stretched from Hungary to Vietnam – the largest nation the world has ever known.

After the demise of the great Khans and the decline of their empire, Mongolians reverted to their former obscurity as nomadic herders and pastoralists. In 1691, Outer Mongolia was also forced to accede to Manchuria and for the next two hundred and twenty years things were grim. Outer Mongolia was occupied by the Chinese army who meted out severe punishment for any insubordination. Meanwhile Chinese traders used usurious practices that kept the naive nomadic cattle breeders permanently in debt.

Early in the twentieth century, when almost all the country was living in poverty, an independence movement grew and the struggle for liberation began. In 1911, with the fall of the Ching dynasty in China, the Mongol princes made a bid for the control of their country. They failed and were forced to accept China's dominance again but, after the Russian revolution in 1917, they asked the Russians for help. In 1921 Russian and Mongolian forces captured Mongolia's capital city and in 1924 Mongolia was proclaimed a people's republic. Serfdom and feudal tax were abolished, but now Mongolia was under Russian domination.

Mongolians lost their religious and social order and needed Russian help for everything. The Russians kept them ignorant and cut off from the world. In 1939 Japan

127

occupied Inner Mongolia, but were soundly thrashed when they attempted to invade Outer Mongolia. When the Soviet Communist Party was ousted in 1991, Russian financial support and military control ceased in Outer Mongolia. The economy, which had been bad even with Russia propping it up – in 1991 one in three people were living below the poverty line – totally disintegrated. Only emergency aid and food from western nations saved the country from total famine. Theft, previously rare, increased, especially of government goods such as railway equipment and telephone cables. Everything was rationed, and every day injuries resulted from fights in the long bread queues.

Today Outer Mongolia is in a state of transition as the government, the Mongolian People's Revolutionary Party, pursue gradual free market economic reforms. The economy remains frail, and there are still drastic shortages of food and basic consumer goods in all areas except the capital, Ulaan Baatar. Even here only meagre and uncertain supplies are available. We visitors had been warned to carry tinned food supplies and all personal articles, especially toilet paper – this precious item was non-existent – with us.

I lunched in the train's dining car in the company of the three other intrepid travellers who shared my closet-sized compartment – Denise, an American woman, Yoshi, an Israeli, and Paul, a New Zealander. A helpful waitress translated the Chinese menu for us, and we ordered several communal plates. The food was good. Rice was cheap at fourteen cents (one *yuan*), but the other dishes were expensive by Chinese standards and beer was exorbitant at five *yuan* for a large bottle. Now and then the train stopped at a station where we hung out of the windows and bought, via the Look and Point system, apples and drinks from healthy, happy looking girls whose red cheeks were the same colour as their apples.

By six in the evening the landscape was almost empty except for an occasional village. The mountain climber in our midst told us that we were now five thousand feet above sea level. Our ears popped, confirming this. Mongolia is one of the highest countries in the world, with an average elevation of 1580 metres.

I ate a delicious mix of eggs and tomatoes and watched the sunset through the dining car window. Above the gentle hills on the horizon a delicate pale pink flush gradually deepened to an orange-red flame until darkness occluded it. There was no heating on the train, but I was wearing all my warm clothes, and so far I had not felt the onslaught of the cold I dreaded.

Our group of thirteen, the Dirty Dozen plus me, were a pleasant lot. Apart from those in my compartment there were five young Japanese – three boys and two girls – a French and a Welsh couple. When I was not socialising with them I lay up in my top bunk and read. In comparison to the super swank Shanghai–Beijing express, this train was shabby but, although the toilets were an abomination, it was functional and comfortable enough.

At ten that night we reached Dzamin Ud, the border post on the Chinese side. Outer Mongolia, landlocked in the centre of the Asian continent, is a big country, the seventeenth largest in the world. It is three times the size of France, covering an area of 1,566,000 square kilometres. It has 7678 kilometres of border but only two neighbours, the Soviet Union in the north and China in the south. The Trans Siberian train is Mongolia's only link with the outside world. There is not even an air mail service – a letter can take two weeks to three months to arrive. No wonder it was possible for the Russians to isolate them.

As I climbed down onto the platform at Dzamin Ud, I was assaulted by disco music, blaring from a nearby loud speaker. The railway station was aptly described by another traveller as resembling a German town hall. It was lit by a gaudy neon sign and strings of coloured lights. It sat square on the barren desert sand, looking out of place in the blowing dust. Before we left the train, our passports were taken from us by a severe female border guard. She said, 'You! Look here!' to one girl who turned her face away as she was being inspected and we were ordered, 'You sit! You stand! You go back inside! You down!' (to me, still in my bunk). After this intimidation it was a relief to come across a platoon of friendly soldiers waiting in the station; some even spoke a little English. One young officer told me that they had been sent here for training, although it seemed more like a punishment post to me. He said that they spend from one to four years in college and learn English, Russian and Japanese.

I went inside the station to look for the bank. I walked upstairs along a poorly lit empty gallery, and emerged into a large, open hall that was utterly deserted. I peered through a small hole in one of the side walls and asked the small bloke hiding in there if he was the money changer. He admitted he was but said there were no *togrogs*, the Mongolian currency, available. So much for the guide book, which swore there would be *togrogs* in abundance at this spot. When you can find them you get about four hundred and fifty for one American dollar. The average family income in Mongolia is around 3200 *togrogs* a month.

In the cold open air behind the station building the temporary stalls of a lively market were doing a roaring trade in what appeared to be mostly beer. No wonder, you could get ten large bottles for eighteen *yuan*. Mountainous piles of boxes containing this popular

130

commodity were stacked around the stalls. Several truck loads of it went aboard the train with Mongolians or Chinese who would sell it at a profit in Ulaan Baatar or beyond. Other goodies, destined for the consumer-starved Mongolians and Siberians, joined us here as well. I saw two ironing boards, a mattress and complete bedding outfit, and a multitude of huge bags and bundles shoved aboard. Mongolians are expert smugglers, and the Russians turn the train into a mobile bazaar once it reaches Siberia.

I wandered around the tiny stalls, which were lit by small kerosene lights strung overhead in rows like fairy lights, giving the market a festive air. I was an object of much curiosity. People stopped what they were doing to stare at me, mouths agape. I bought some bananas at an inflated price – we were almost in Outer Mongolia after all – and a red-skinned sausage that for all its lurid looks tasted horribly bland. Its red plastic cover might have had more flavour, but for once I failed to eat the wrappings.

We waited in the station for two and a half hours while the train was driven into a huge workshop to have its wheels changed. China and Russia have different-sized railway lines to prevent easy access for an invasion. As I sat talking to the friendly Chinese army officer, I counted fifteen station hands as they sauntered past and there were more outside – all for one train each way per week. What did they do in between?

Whatever it was, they were smartly decked out to do it; both their fawn uniforms and peaked caps were weighed down by gold braid, stars, shiny buttons and sundry embellishments. As well as the station hands, there were six army officers on duty. There were probably more back at the barracks in bed – which is where I wished I was, though not necessarily the same one!

The piercing scream of a whistle and the chug of a diesel engine announced the welcome return of the train.

Back on board our passports were returned to us. We travelled a few kilometres to the Mongolian border post where we went through it all, except the wheels bit, again. A pretty Mongolian officer, whose pale face was embellished by make up and lipstick, but whose expression and manner were stern, made us fill out customs and immigration forms. I was dying to sleep, but she inspected the cabin at length. To the occupants of the lower berths she said, 'You! Out!' and lifted each bunk to see if we were smuggling any Chinese into the country. Then she closely inspected us, our luggage, and the luggage compartment up the top. She even made those wearing glasses take them off to compare them with their photos. Anyone who even remotely resembles their passport photo has a lot to worry about.

An hour later the train was finally allowed to leave, and we could go to sleep. It was half-past one in the morning.

We rocked gently through the night. I slept soundly and rose eager for breakfast. At the border the utilitarian Chinese dining car had been changed for a more upmarket Mongolian one. The car boasted vinyl upholstered benches, blinds, imitation flowers in big glass vases and no wine but wine holders filled with imitation flowers (some substitute!). There was an extensive menu in English, Mongolian and Chinese, but nothing was available except 'stroganoff'. As an added bonus, the plate in front of me bore traces of the remains of someone's egg. I flicked a dead fly off the tablecloth and swapped the plate for the cleaner one next door, which left a big black ring on the cloth.

The stroganoff, even though it was nothing like

stroganoff, was surprisingly good; a heap of chopped mutton, rice, fried potato and onion, pickled cabbage and slices of dill pickle and hard fried egg. I was hungry and I thought it was delicious.

The serving was big enough for a navvy and there was strong coffee to follow. My breakfast cost six dollars, which probably explained why there were five restaurant staff and no customers except me. I paid in *yuan*, the maitre d' converted this to American dollars and gave me my change in *togrogs*. I felt I lost something in the exchange.

Having dealt with the important issue of food, I turned my attention to where we were. Looking out the window, I saw the undulating land of the Gobi desert, which occupies most of the southern third of Mongolia. Although arid and semi-barren, the Gobi still has abundant wildlife, including rare species such as the khavtgai wild camel, wild ass, mazalai bear and black-tailed antelope, and it sustains nomadic herders with their flocks of camels and goats. Summers in the Gobi are baking hot. It is normal for the temperature to reach forty degrees Celsius, but the nights can drop to minus thirty.

Mongolia is a land of natural contrasts as well as extremes of weather. It has wild, remote northern forests, permanent glaciers, Siberian steppes, alpine meadows, snow-clad mountains, vast plains and grasslands, and, in the south, the desert. The northernmost half of the country, where the temperature can drop to fifty-two degrees Celsius below freezing, is covered in permafrost. The south, owing to the high mountain ranges that surround it on nearly all sides, has a continental climate, and in the area between the two, Siberian style winters are the norm. Mongolia is also a land of winds and devastating storms, especially on the steppes and in the Gobi. Mongolia has retained vast areas of unspoiled virgin country as a result of its low population and its limited industrialisation. Although the soil is rich in minerals – coal, iron, copper, tungsten, phosphorites, gold, silver, tin, zinc and fluorspar – they are largely unexploited.

Early in the day the train stopped at a couple of small dreary towns. These consisted of a few ugly box like buildings, from which people in Mongolian dress and boots emerged to sell goods through the train windows. They sold potatoes and *khoumis*, fermented mare's milk, which is a Mongolian national treat. The vendors poured the drink from a thermos into a communal cup from which the customers all drank. I opted to make tea with the hot water provided by a coal-fired samovar that steamed away at the end of the train corridor.

Children came down to the line to watch the train pass through each village. They looked well fed and clothed and friendly enough, but were frequently armed with shanghais, and they took pot shots at the train as it went by. One of our windows scored a direct hit, but fortunately only the outer window of the double glazing was smashed. The dogs that accompanied the kids looked strong and had thick shaggy coats, resembling huskies. Being opportunists like all dogs, they begged scraps from the passengers when the train was stopped. It was strange to see dogs kept as pets and shepherds again after the total absence of them in China.

We were well into Outer Mongolia now, travelling across the central grasslands where open treeless plains spread to the far distance. The green grass of summer was turning brown and the dry landscape reminded me of Australia. The railway followed an endless line of telegraph wires that swung between poles roughly cut from tree trunks. Occasionally we passed herds of horses and small groups of Bactrian camels that cantered away from the train with an awkward knock-kneed motion. Their two strange lopsided humps looked like the camels had had a nasty accident.

I saw the first round white roofs of *yurts*, or *gers* as they are called in Mongolian. *Yurt* is Russian, and all that is Russian is now on the outer in Mongolia. If you said *yurt*, Mongolians looked at you as though you had uttered a dirty word. From a distance *gers* looked like the grain silos you find on Australian farms. There are only three large cities in Mongolia – Ulaan Baatar, Darkhan and Erdenet – and almost all the people outside them live in *gers* – circular portable tents with pixie cap tops.

There were long intervals between railway stations. These lonely places on the infinite steppes consisted of two or three rectangular brick buildings with a wooden stockade for the animals and a sheet of water lying in a depression where long-horned cattle browsed. A few people would appear to watch the train go past. I saw a few worn tracks next to the railway line, but no vehicles. Then the tracks petered out and there was nothing, only grass-covered emptiness.

Later there were bigger herds of horses – some of the two million plus that Mongolia boasts. Mongolia's horse population is equal in amount to its population of just over two million people – 1.3 per square kilometre. It is one of the most sparsely occupied countries on earth. While other countries quote statistics in head of livestock per population, Mongolia does it the other way around. There are thirteen or more sheep for every person, and the total of twenty-five and a half million animals is ten times the number of people.

Hours passed and I still looked out into deserted land relieved only infrequently by signs of life; an eagle circling high overhead, horses grazing, a camel rider silhouetted against the clear blue sky, a couple of *gers*, horsemen watching us go by, or galloping against the wind holding the noose and pole they use for lassooing animals. The Mongols have lived as nomadic livestock breeders and herders for seven to eight thousand years, raising horses, sheep, goats, camels and cattle. The steppes in the east and west are splendid pastures, but the difficult climate necessitated constant migration. The Mongolian ideals – respect for independence, reverence for the spirit of the earth, and traditions of hospitality and friendliness – were formed by their hard, nomadic life. Almost all aspects of society still revolve around pastoral life. The Russians introduced some state farms in an attempt to grow crops of grain and introduce vegetables into the Mongolians' diet, but in the harsh climate it was high-risk farming. Crops were doubtful and most Mongols flatly refuse to eat vegetables, saying they are animals' food and quoting the old proverb 'Meat for men, leaves for animals'.

During the nomadic Mongols' history they also built grandiose cities, now all erased by time and cataclysms. At Karakorum, where the trade routes met in 1220 AD, Ghenghis Khan built the Palace of Universal Peace. Covering 2475 square metres, its forecourt sported a solid silver fountain shaped like a tree with four silver lions belching out *khoumis* at its base, while from the top, wine, *khoumis* and rice beer spurted from the open mouths of silver snakes. This ostentatious treasure was reputed to have been built by Master Wilhelm of Paris. Craftsmen and artists from many countries were imported to contribute to the palace wonders.

An hour or so from our destination the train tracks ran through soft brown hills that rolled away like folds of felt. Several *gers* clustered in the bottom of a dell, along with a small group of cattle and a large mob of about five hundred sheep, dun-coloured and long tailed, up to their black faces in waving grass.

A lone hawk circled the edge of the railway line, hoping we might stir up a meal for him. Hawking is still a favoured sport of the nomads. The hills gave way to mountains, fold on fold of them ranked behind each other, as we climbed higher. Finally the odd tree joined the landscape, first birch, then pine or fir, and an occasional copse of deciduous trees glowing autumnal yellow.

12 My *ger*

At last we came to Ulaan Baatar, 1561 kilometres from Beijing. In the outskirts of the town we passed through extensive suburbs of *gers* that were surrounded by fences of rough, wooden planks nailed side by side. The rest of the town consisted of box-like apartments resembling barracks and a few tall buildings, which I presumed to be in the inner city. I read an article in the local paper that said no more of these Russian-style apartments were to be built and that *gers* would be the housing from now on.

I alighted on the platform at the same time as a Mongolian bearing a complete brass bed. The railway station was designed in 'Soviet heavy style' but we did not get inside it. We were rounded up on the platform by our keeper and immediately diverted to the street.

Dutifully trooping after our guide, a good-looking, long and lithe young Mongolian called BB, we were shunted into a mini-bus. We immediately set off for the camp in the Teralj, eighty kilometres away in the Hentii Nuruu mountains, where we were to spend the next five days. Passing through the great, wide streets of Ulaan Baatar, I saw cows and horses grazing unchaperoned on the footpaths and people in bright Mongolian dress. The streets, which seemed deserted after China's hordes, were dotted here and there with trees and shrubs.

The good road ended shortly after we left the city. We were bounced along an uneven, one-car-wide strip of bitumen through country where large herds of livestock roamed. Soon the hills began. They had soft, carpet-like surfaces, but were mainly treeless. As we climbed higher, the hills became small mountains. The trees increased, and the hilltops became more and more stony until some were entirely weathered rock. Then we were among the towering peaks of huge mountains, their slopes covered with groves of deciduous trees in autumn shades. As we drove deep down into valleys and climbed up out again, we passed *gers* nestled in small groups in the sheltering arms of cosy glens. And once we saw several yaks, huge and lumbering, being driven across a pasture by a man on horseback.

Turning off the bitumen onto a bone-shaking dirt track, we eventually came to the camp. Five *gers*, surrounded by forest and encircled by imposing mountains, squatted snugly on the small valley floor. Close to them skulked a hideous, Russian built monstrosity. It was erected as a rest house for civil servants and military nobs. This building was where we were to be fed, watered and washed during our stay in the *gers*. Executed in the manner thought to be grand in Soviet circles, and probably palatial by local standards, the building had floors of marble tiles and very broad corridors. Down the centre of these and up the marble staircase ran an elegant dark-red patterned carpet. The stairs had been built without a balustrade, but one had been added as an afterthought, possibly after some vodka-soaked politician had stepped off the side.

The entire establishment was squeaky clean. After

China, I had expected Mongolia to be putrid. I even saw the cook washing the corridor walls in between meals. The only staff of the establishment were the kitchen workers – two women and a man – who doubled as cleaners.

Although the sun was shining and the sky was brilliant blue, the weather had grown cold as we entered the mountains and we needed our down coats and woollies. On our arrival we were taken into this winter palace and given dinner before being allocated our *gers*. The dining room was large and institutional, like an army mess, with long tables surrounded by chairs. We ate borsch soup without beetroot, but with vegetables, mutton and sour cream – luscious. It was followed by mutton rissoles shaped like sausages, potatoes, rice and freshly baked bread, accompanied by several large thermoses of tea. This was our first taste of the dreaded mutton we had been constantly warned about. I don't know why everyone complains. I like it.

The bathroom in the winter palace was a bleak frozen grotto with permanently open windows. Just what I needed – more freezing fresh air. There was one cold shower which did not seem to have seen too much action, but Paul, the New Zealand boy, one of our more hardy souls, used it once. Those who didn't want a cold shower had to resort to a cold wash at the row of communal hand basins, in full view of everyone. There was no segregation of the sexes, which even extended to the never vacant three toilets. I performed my ablutions in my *ger* by pouring hot water from the large thermos provided for tea into my travelling plastic cereal bowl, dipping my face washer in it and wiping around my visible edges – making a mental note to sterilise the bowl later.

Gers were really tents that could be collapsed, transported and reassembled. They were originally built on carts – the huge ones for the nobility were built on platforms drawn by twenty-two oxen. I made myself at home in my *ger*. The gaily painted wooden door, which always faced south to the sun, was so small I had to bend over to get in, but once inside the place was a joy. It was a very effective, compact, strong, cosy portable house that appealed to my nomadic instincts.

Gers had only one circular wall supported by a frame of narrow latticed birch willow boards, laced together with leather strips and hair rope. So that they could be moved these boards could be folded like an accordion or an umbrella and were covered with two thick felt layers topped with an overcoat of canvas. In the summer, layers could be removed or the lower part raised to let in the air. Apart from the door, the only opening was a plastic-covered peephole in the centre of the roof through which the stove flue protruded and light and air were admitted when required. A canvas cover could be rolled over the opening by pulling the hair rope that hung from it and to which a stone weight could be attached as a stabiliser in high winds. From the centre of the peaked roof, wooden supports spread like the spines of a fan, very close together at the top and about eight inches apart where they met the side supports. The wooden floor of my *ger* was covered with a layer of felt, except at the entrance where slatted boards formed a porch so that you didn't walk straight in off the dirt or snow, and around the stove where lino ensured you didn't burn the place down. The average *ger* provided sixteen to eighteen metres of living space, but bigger ones were used in towns for clubs, libraries, cafes and bars.

In the middle of the *ger*, between the four centre supports, was the hearth. Called the parental hearth, it was sacred, as was fire, and symbolised ties with your ancestors. Desecration of the hearth was a sin and an insult to the master of the house. The taboos of the hearth included: pouring water on it, stepping over it, spilling milk on it, stretching your legs towards it, throwing rubbish in the stove, or bringing sharp objects close to the fire. It was forbidden to touch or lean on the central supports – they formed a link with heaven, the past, present and the future. The stove was mounted on three stones representing the host, hostess and daughter-in-law – who was special because she was the mother of the heir. The *ger* was divided into three spaces – male, female and *khoimor* – the guest space opposite the door, which I interpreted as neutral territory.

The western side, under the protection of heaven, was the male area, and here the owner hung his saddle, bridle and *khoumis* bag. The eastern side, where the kitchenware and children's belongings were kept, claimed the protection of the sun and belonged to the females. Furniture was standard; intricately carved and painted chests and shelves. Weapons, the *morin khuur* – a traditional musical instrument similar to a guitar with a handle carved like a horse's head – and two chests were kept in the neutral territory while the bed, with the Buddhist altar placed just to the right of it, was in the female quarters. Children went to sleep at their parents' feet.

Inside my *ger* everything was brilliantly decorated and painted. The wooden roof supports were bright vermilion and orange with patterns picked out in gold, as were the enclosed beds that were rather like the bunks you get on a ship. The top end of the bed formed a shelf on which to put your night time refreshments, and beside it were two little cupboards. Near the hearth a low, bow-legged table was surrounded by four tiny stools all decorated in the same way. Wood was used for the fire when it was available. If it wasn't, horse, cow or other animal dung became fuel, especially in the Gobi where there were no trees.

My bed had no mattress, merely two layers of felt laid on the slatted board base, a bit hard on the bits of my hips that had no padding. To cover me I had a thick quilt inside a cotton doona cover and a heavy felt blanket on top of that. The pillow was a small square object that was possibly filled with lead.

People living in the *gers* were usually friendly and would invite in strangers, even tourists, and give them yoghurt, cheese, tea and *khoumis*. You do not knock at a *ger* door, but as you approach it shout, 'Hold the dog!' Male guests take snuff from each other's snuff boxes and then return them. Tea would be handed to you with the right hand while the left hand held the right elbow. You received the cup in the same manner, mindful of the fact that it was impolite to take anything while exposing your wrists. In summer a large cup of *khoumis* would be served. It was customary to eat and drink from a common plate and cup as an indication of trust towards the host.

It did not get dark until eight o'clock and the weather remained tolerable until the sun went down. Then it suddenly got very cold. After dinner I lit my fire, and after a quick nip outside to admire the smoke curling lazily out of the *ger* roof, I hibernated until morning. The small stove in the centre of my *ger* did a fine job, heating the place almost immediately.

The night was very still. There was no need for the ear plugs I had found necessary to preserve my sanity in China. It was so peaceful I wanted to listen to the quiet. But was it cold! I went to bed with the fire burning and slept solidly. I woke once during the night to the sound of rain beating on the peephole's plastic and a steady drip of water falling somewhere inside. I thought that I should get out and put something under the leak, but I wasn't brave enough to face the cold. Next time I woke it was seven o'clock, the first light was beginning to show and the air in the *ger* was glacial. I leaped out of bed, lit the fire, and jumped back in as quickly as I could. Snuggling down luxuriously in my warm bed, I listened to the sound of rain spattering on the roof, while a large bird called raucously outside.

Soon the temperature was bearable. I had my cereal bowl wash, but it was too cold to take off my clothes and replace them with the icy ones that had lain out on the spare bed overnight and were so cold they felt wet. So I put more layers on top of what I was already wearing – an acceptable local practice. The next night I hung my clothes on a line near the stove so I would have something warmer to put on in the morning.

By the time I was respectable it was nine o'clock and the breakfast trough was ready, thank goodness. They held the morning feeding at a decent hour. You certainly wouldn't want to get up any earlier in this climate.

Until now, the only cars I had seen in Mongolia were a couple of battered Russian ones. But now a reasonably new Mercedes rocked up and disgorged some fat cat male Mongolian politicians into the winter palace. They arrived wearing old-fashioned western suits of the Kremlin cut, but when they reappeared shortly afterwards they had changed into their national dress. They set off on foot towards the mountains. Our guide, BB, which could stand for a lot of things in Australian – he refused to tell us his name or anything else for that matter – broke his silence for once and told me that the politicians had gone up the mountain to chop down a tree and have a Mongolian barbecue. I concluded after a while that BB was an angry young man who was jealous of the wealth and freedom of westerners.

144

Breakfast consisted of sweetened barley gruel in milk – filling is the best you could say about it – one cold boiled egg and bread and jam.

Outside I found a Mongolian man with a cluster of horses he hoped to hire out. He wore traditional gear: long black leather boots, trousers covered by a knee-length wrap over robe that was circled by a broad sash, and a round peaked hat sat on the back of his head. His face was extremely weathered, but it was not a bad-looking face and he had a genuine, warm smile. From the way he handled horses it was obvious that he was an expert horseman, which earned my respect.

The three Japanese boys, who I don't think had seen a horse before, and I, were the only fearless riders. They because they did not realise the dangers, and I because I was mad enough to get on any horse. The horses were in marvellous condition. Although their coats were rough and they were unshod, they were well fed, almost fat, and there were no sores on them, unlike the poor beasts in China.

Mongolians love horses, and their culture revolves around them. The national emblem depicts a galloping horseman, signifying freedom and independence. The horse is considered a symbol of glory and splendour and it is said that 'The sight of a good horse reinvigorates the spirit'. I agreed. I never saw an ugly horse. The *Tah*, or Przevalski horse, the forebear of the modern horse, was prevalent in Mongolia until it was hunted to near extinction. It had been bred in captivity in the west, however, and had been recently reintroduced to its primeval home in the grasslands of Mongolia.

One of the reasons for my fascination with Mongolia was the legendary horsemanship of the people. When I was a child I saw Jack Palance being mean as Ghenghis Khan in an old film and he, and the stupendous feats of his hordes as they thundered across the steppes, won my undying regard for this country and its people.

Our horses ranged in colour from dun to brown and black. They were really only ponies and although I chose the biggest, he was still just the size of a small horse and had a very short gait. The horseman told us to shout, 'Choo!' to get the horses moving. He sang softly to himself as we got underway. He should be happy. For this little jaunt he earned forty American dollars, which was almost equivalent to the Mongolian national debt. He sang louder and the boys began to copy him, so he taught us a Mongolian riding song. My saddle was small, but not uncomfortable. It was made of two pieces of wood on an iron frame, which rested on a cotton pad laid on the horse's back on which a thick cotton cushion was placed. The bridle and reins were leather, and the iron stirrups were tied on with rope. My horse proved quiet, bomb-proof in fact, and slow to get moving. Even when I did manage to get him going – I plucked a piece of passing tree and used it as an accelerator – he only did a speedy trot, not a canter. Mongols usually rode at a fast, sitting trot. That was what the horseman did so I copied him.

It was glorious to ride through the amazing scenery. We passed under an enormous rock formation that consisted of a pair of colossal, smooth stones, one balanced high on the other a hundred metres in the air – like the Devil's Marbles near Tenant Creek in Central Australia, only much bigger.

After a short while we left the road, and I could ride faster over the grasslands that lay before the mountains and the forest. The sound of the horses' unshod hooves went from a muted clip clop on the dirt road, to a pounding thud as I sprinted over the thick green grass.

The Mongols firmly believe that 'mountain areas, especially in summer and autumn, have their own magical power to purify the mist in the human mind and heart'. Well, it was autumn, and I was prepared to believe the saying too. It was magnificent country. The leaves on the mountain trees were all changing colour: bright butter yellow to pale lemon and russet to rusty gold. They shone in a kaleidoscope of hues against the gentle browns and greens of the hills. With only the sound of our muffled hoof beats breaking the silence, we rode through an enchanted forest. The slim trees grew so close together that they covered us with their canopy, and the earth was thickly layered with fallen leaves, round and neat and golden, as though the fortune of a royal treasury had been showered here. It was pure magic. Under the roof of shimmering jewelled leaves, in the dappled dreamy light, we seemed to be in King Arthur country. I *know* this was what Camelot was like.

After climbing very high, we took a short cut back, almost straight down a precipitous mountain. At the mountain summit, the horseman indicated that we should dismount. He took my horse and gave me his whip. It had a very strong handle, and I got the message that it was a steep descent, and I was to use the whip as a staff. He was right. I had to tread very carefully. The shining leaves underfoot made a slide straight to the bottom and a broken neck a good possibility. I could not have held the horse on this descent; it would have pulled me over.

Next we were in an open valley trotting through waving silvery grass. We travelled a long way, stopping now and then to give the horses a drink from one of the creeks we crossed. One of the Japanese boys allowed his horse to start drinking from a stagnant pool, but the horseman said, 'No! No!' He would only let them drink running water. We rode past several small settlements of *gers* and passed through a herd of cows and their attendant bull, a white creature with massive horns. The cows, and the small flocks of sheep we saw, were guarded from wolves by fierce dogs that looked remarkably wolf-like themselves. Wolves were on the increase in Mongolia, where there were reported to be thirty to forty thousand. I saw a few black crows but none of the snakes that we had been told were so prevalent in this area, nor, to my disappointment, any bears or wolves. But we did see a few ground squirrels and a *tarvaga*, a marmot, a furry creature, similar to a prairie dog, common in Mongolia. I had already seen them from the train and the bus. The *tarvagas* are extremely useful; their flesh is tender and good to eat, their fur is good quality and the three-inch layer of fat that keeps them warm is used for medicinal purposes.

Mongols worship nature and their ancestors. They have always had a careful attitude to the environment, and ninety-five per cent of Mongolia is ecologically clean. It remains the most pristine country in Asia. The mountain range that towers over Ulaan Baatar has been a protected area for almost two hundred years. No rivers flow into the country, so the water in the three thousand eight hundred rivers and streams and four thousand lakes remain uncontaminated. And as there is no commercial fishing – Mongolians won't eat fish – the waterways teem with salmon, trout, sturgeon and greenfish.

Ten per cent of Mongolia is covered by forests of conifers, larch, cedar, pine, fir and spruce, and deciduous trees such as birch, aspen, and poplar. There are also willows, ledum, bird cherry, honeysuckle, rose willow, briar and hawthorn. Above the forest line there are high altitude meadows, where you can pick an edelweiss without risking your neck on a mountain.

The Mongolian guelder rose and the Mongolian adonis are protected plants, but there are more than five hundred species of plant life. Valuable extracts are taken from herbs, fruits and berries to be used medicinally in the pharmacies.

Mongolia is home to one hundred and forty mammal species, three hundred and ninety species of birds, twenty kinds of reptile and seventy-six varieties of fish. The northern forests are home to maral and roe as well as northern and musk deer. Wild boar are found everywhere and fur-bearing animals are plentiful – glutton, fox, corsac, lynx, ermine, Siberian weasel, sable, brown bears, snow leopard and wolves. The argali mountain ram and the yangir mountain goat are found in some mountain areas. Foreign hunters visit the country to shoot for sport because of the prolific wildlife. In the forests there are birds in abundance: mountain ouzels, blackbirds, wood grouse and black grouse. White swans, pelicans and cormorants are found on rivers and lakes, while the steppes have grey cranes, bustards, eagles, white-tailed sea eagles, hawks, falcons, harriers and black griffons. Fifty rare animals and seventy plants are on the verge of extinction in Mongolia – the mazalai bear, the Przevalski horse, the Mongolian saiga, the khavtgai wild camel, the Mongolian wild ass, the Ussuri elk, the red wolf, the Altai mountain ram, and the irbis or snow leopard.

13 More mutton

After the long, three hour ride it was good to return to the dining room for a filling lunch of mutton. This time it skulked under a layer of potato trying to pretend it was shepherd's pie.

After lunch I saw the Mongolian gentry ride off on the horses we had ridden that morning. It started to rain again so I went into my *ger*, lit the fire. and lay down on my bed with a book. The *ger* was soon pleasantly warm, and I listened happily to the rain falling gently on the roof and the wind rustling lightly in the trees.

The young Welsh couple in our group came to visit. They were returning home after travelling up from the south of China. They told me there was a way you could cross overland into North Vietnam at the Chinese border near Kunming. It sounded difficult but not impossible. I decided to try it. Then the charming French couple came in complaining that their wood had run out and that they were freezing. I had thought that the others would tolerate the cold better than I. They'd had more practice.

Without the fire, I would have been miserable although

my down overcoat helped to make the weather bearable. Even out riding it had kept out the cold, but it was so bulky that once I had my arms in the sleeves, I couldn't reach down to do it up. I had to tie it together by the strings in the middle or ask someone to help me. It was like an old-fashioned eiderdown – light but cumbersome – and wearing it I felt as though I was wrapped in a mattress and a double bedspread.

There were also two Japanese girl students in our group whom I nicknamed Miki and Moto. The shyer of the two celebrated her birthday while we were at the camp. At dinner we presented her with a card we had all signed and, as we couldn't find any candles, we lit three sticks of kindling for her to blow out while we sang happy birthday.

Every day someone filled the wood box that stood next to the stove in my *ger*. It was then up to me to set and light the fire. Before I went to bed I would get ready for the morning, laying the fire and organising my Water Management Program. I would fill the big thermos from the huge samovar in the kitchen and put it next to my cereal bowl. BB said that these big thermoses were the only good thing that the Chinese had introduced to Mongolia. (They don't like the Chinese any more than the Russians.) I became proficient at the fire-making business and came to quite enjoy it. But it was hard to find enough paper to start a blaze. I used all sorts of odd things, like the crossword puzzle I had been carrying with me since Darwin and had finally finished, the wrapping off the toilet roll and the cardboard from the middle of it. I never used the roll itself, it was too precious, my entire supply having been carried from China. I got accustomed to always carrying loo paper. As the jingle goes, you can't leave home without it.

The winter palace was locked after dark, so unless

you wanted to expose your sensitive parts to the cold night air and the bears and wolves, you had to make a portable loo by cutting a plastic bottle in half. There was no electric power, and it was still almost dark when I got up in the mornings. I would grab my torch, throw on my overcoat and hurriedly light the fire. Then I would jump back into bed to watch the reflections of the glowing flames dance on the brilliant colours inside the *ger*. I would wallow in my warm bed and plan my Getting Up Campaign – how and what to throw on first before the cold hit me.

On our last morning in the camp, I untied the leather thong that secured my door from the inside, and stopped in amazement. It was snowing! Flakes of snow, light and fine, floated soundlessly down and lay thick on the ground. By lunch time the whole world was white. The trees were frosted over. The mountains behind the camp had disappeared; only a few brown rocks hinted that there was anything out there at all. Visibility was limited to a few feet, as a haze of swirling snowflakes obscured everything. Icicles hung from under the eaves of the winter palace, which now truly lived up to its name. A heavy mass of snow sat solidly on the roofs of the *gers*, making them look like iced cakes.

At three in the afternoon we set off into a snow-white world to return to Ulaan Baatar. The bus driver somehow found his way, skidding and slipping, not on the dirt road that was now invisible, but by following his nose. Even when we came to the main road it seemed dangerous. I wished I had not read that Mongolia's road toll for the last three months had been fifty-four dead and one hundred and fifty-eight injured. I saw a marmot going about his business in the snow, a horseman – a dramatic black silhouette against the white background – and cows that stood with a layer of snow on their backs. When the mountains gave way to the rolling hills, the world was entirely white. I could only guess where the hills ended and the sky began by a place on the horizon that had a greyish look. We passed a car bogged by the side of the road. Two sturdy horses and a horseman had been recruited to pull it out. The white sides and roofs of a group of *gers* disappeared into the background; only the vermilion and orange wooden doors gave them away.

The windscreen wipers on our bus stopped working, but this did not slow the driver in the least. I was nervous. The day before a Mongolian International Air Transport MIAT plane had crashed, killing all its passengers. That's why I won't fly! But even this bus travel was looking dicey right now.

It was still snowing when we reached Ulaan Baatar. The streets were lined with snow-trimmed trees and a carpet of crisp white flakes lay underfoot. We were taken to the Ulaan Baatar Hotel so that we could at last obtain some *togrogs*. The UB, as it was known locally, looked quite a decent hotel, but it was not for us. We were taken miles out to the suburbs and into the former Russian ghetto to our 'hotel'. What a dump. A couple of daggy old flats that had been chopped up into mass accommodation. It boasted the dubious convenience of a prostitute who lived on the floor above us. Our group were the only guests, and the staff consisted of one young, female Mongolian with no English. She was the cook, housemaid and chief bottle washer.

The hotel's one redeeming feature was that it was clean. But it was not, as guaranteed, a good hotel, with bathrooms and heating. I had to fight for an extra blanket, one per bed was the regulation issue. And it was snowing outside!

My room was next to the bathroom – which was understandable, as my room had originally been the kitchen.

I slept with my head nearly in the porcelain kitchen sink which, complete with the stainless steel draining board, occupied a large amount of the tiny room. One half of the drainer had been roughly chopped off, leaving jagged, metal edges. The single bed was crammed against it. There was only enough space in this room for the bed and the sink. A naked light bulb hung from the ceiling in my room, but I had to go into the corridor to turn it on or off. For decoration I had all the water pipes around the tiled walls, a coffee table and a red plush velvet ottoman. There were no curtains or blinds. I pinched a sheet from the room next door, which had a spare bed, and covered the window to keep out the cold, as well as to prevent the management selling tickets outside to watch me disrobe. The bed had a bullet-filled pillow.

The door to my room could not be shut without first removing the key from the outside lock to re-lock it from the inside. If I stood on the ottoman, a long narrow window high on the interior wall gave, for a reason that completely eluded me, a vista into the bathroom next door. I told my companions I could take pictures of them in the shower to put on my Christmas cards. They were strangely reluctant. Unfortunately this trick could be performed from both sides, so I was restrained by their counter threats to capture me on film. I imagined being asked what kind of a view my hotel room in Mongolia had. 'Oh, my window opened into the bathroom. I had great views!'

The bathroom had no light, nor did the toilet next to it, where even during the day it was pitch black. The only night time illumination for the bathroom came from my light, through the window in my room. But other unsuspecting guests naturally presumed that my light switch in the corridor was for the bathroom, with dire results for me.

I passed a miserable night. The bed springs poked through the mattress into my hips no matter how I lay, and the pillow hurt my head. Although I wore long underwear, two T-shirts, a long woolly nightie and a jumper, and had my down overcoat on top of the two blankets, I was chilled to the bone. Someone decided to go to the toilet and turned on the switch in the corridor. I was almost asleep. One thousand watts blasted me full in the face. From then the light continued to go on and off like a lighthouse beacon until I was wide awake and livid. Were all my companions night owls with bladder problems? Finally I got to sleep, only to be woken at five in the morning as the light once again flashed in my face. The toilet was, of course, faulty, and sounded in need of plumbing repairs. Once flushed, it continued to run. There was another peculiar high window between the bathroom and the loo which enabled me to hear all the action in there too.

But it was a lovely day. The sun was shining, the sky was a heavenly blue and the air was as clear as a bell. The soft snow of yesterday had packed down hard and crunched like sugar when I walked on it. Too cold for it to melt, it remained on the ground for days. Icicles still hung under buses in the street later that afternoon. It was freezing. My breath steamed. From my window on the fourth floor I looked out on the slope of a green hill and, behind that, mountains covered with snow. The top of the hill was level with me and on the very tip I could see three *gers* sheltered from the bitter winds by a circular stockade of wooden planks. Nearby were two big piles of stones with blue pennants flying from poles on their peaks. I saw these cairns frequently. They were part of the animistic religion that had survived, and were situated on top of a hill or on a mountain pass where people could offer praises to nature and the spirit of

155

the mountain or the district. The blue pennants were symbols of kind thoughts and best wishes with which Mongolians honoured each other and nature. On the new year holiday, the pennants were given to guests and family members.

On my hill cows wandered and grazed and at times a pack of six or seven dogs loped around on it, intent on their business. A German Shepherd rambled up the hill, tail curved over his back, looking for his mates. He was joined by a smaller huskie dog and they frisked about on the green grass together. Crows and pigeons flapped about outside my window and one fat pigeon landed on the sill, put his head on one side and gave me the eye. Early in the morning a horseman trotted past the building at a smart pace. On the ground below sparrows bathed in a pool of melted snow and chirped cheerfully in the sun. Listening to them I realised that they sounded the same everywhere; with a warm feeling of familiarity they evoked memories of home. Beneath my window children played in the bare asphalt courtyard. A visitor's horse was tied to the fence and one small girl was picking weed offerings and feeding them to it lovingly.

14 Rapunzel, Rapunzel!

Outside the apartment block, in the frozen snow, a soldier cranked a reluctant army jeep as we, like Good Little Tourists, trooped into our bus to visit Gandantegchinlin, the only monastery that remained functioning. It was bitterly cold. But my overcoat kept most of me warm and more than complied with the rule that decent clothes, with sleeves covering the wrists, be worn when visiting monasteries and temples. Only a couple of inches of my very cold face was exposed.

In 1938 Mongolia had seven hundred and sixty-seven monastic centres containing over five thousand temples and pagodas. Most of these were destroyed when religion was suppressed by the communist government. Once, one hundred thousand of the six hundred thousand Mongolians were monks. In 1991 the BBC reported that a mass burial site containing the skulls of five thousand lamas, executed in the 1930s, had been unearthed in northern Mongolia. This was officially denied.

Before the revolution, Mongolia had some of the world's foremost Buddhist buildings. Many of these exemplified grand steppe architecture – Tibetan and

Chinese styles combined with Mongol, in which archi-
tects often used the shape of the *ger* for inspiration. Its
silhouette is still used in modern constructions.

The Gandantegchinlin monastery, a huge complex
incorporating several enormous temples, was crowded
with devout worshippers following a form of Tibetan
Buddhism, or Lamaism. Numerous monks wearing
maroon and saffron robes sat in rows around an open
square with an altar at one end, chanting Tibetan while
holding narrow, long Tibetan prayer books. Clouds of
incense streamed upwards amid a riot of colourful bells,
pennants and flags. Worshippers, petitioning providence,
presented offerings of money and joss sticks, reverently
holding them forth with both hands and placing them on
the monk's open books. Two fresh-faced teenage monks
turned face to face and chanted fast at each other in
friendly competition until they both dissolved in giggles.
One temple contained a large group of novices under
instruction, some of them only little boys. Another
temple's roof was fashioned entirely from shining brass,
with massive brass bells on each corner. It housed a
gigantic standing Buddha that dwarfed us all.

In the 1920s few people except priests were literate,
but learning the oral history of the family and tribe was,
and still is, an important part of Mongol tradition. Some
family chronicles date back to the eighth century AD.
With the coming of Buddhism many prodigious literary
works were compiled, written in books made up of long
sheets inscribed vertically, stacked together, pressed
between two wooden plates and wrapped in silk. One
religious work that was translated and published was the
Kanjur, an eight-volume epic containing one thousand,
one hundred and sixty-one works. Another totalled three
hundred and thirty-four volumes, each of five hundred
pages, which took three hundred thousand cut boards to

print. The text of each page was framed with precious stones. The first western books to be translated and published in the Mongolian script, which is beautifully decorative and written from the left down the page, were *The Decameron*, *Robinson Crusoe*, Poe's *Gold Bug* and Jules Verne's *Dick Sands*. One of the many rare books in the Ulaan Baatar library is the ten-volume *Sandui Djud Sutra*, which used fifty kilograms of gold and forty kilograms of silver for illustrations and decorations. Another is the masterpiece, *The Secret History of the Mongols*, an extract from which says, 'The high organisational level and discipline that distinguished Mongolian society rested on tribal and inter-tribal solidarity and democratic relations between people.'

At the monastery gates vendors sold charms, religious icons and small bags of grain that people bought for the waiting pigeons. Worshippers walked around huge great bells, ritually touching smaller bells as they went. Others spun Tibetan prayer bells and wheels, and then made a *wei* like the Thais do, by putting their hands together in prayer in front of their faces and bowing. Devotees also walked in a ritual manner around *saburgans* – shrines that bore inscriptions to deities – and placed their foreheads on a special spot marked by a banner as they went by. Others prostrated themselves on the slanting boards that lay on the ground in front of various venerable objects or, as a final act of homage, leaned their heads against the gate posts on their way out of the monastery.

Later in our stay Denise, my American friend, and I returned to the monastery in the late afternoon when most of the crowds had gone. It was pleasant then to sit on a wall and meditate.

The next stop was the natural history museum. Its interesting collection was housed in a 1950s Russian structure and its grand pieces were two dinosaur skeletons that had been found in the Gobi desert. Fully erect, they loomed over you from a great height. The stuffed animal collection was good too, although some were really stuffed in every sense of the word, being moth-eaten and more than slightly the worse for wear. The snakes all had split skins, and some species of the bird collection were seriously moulting. Looking down from an upstairs window into the museum courtyard below, I saw, instead of the garden or statues I expected, only a patch of overgrown grass where a man was dismantling a jeep.

Moving on, we visited what BB called the 'empty department store'. But supplies had improved lately and it wasn't as barren as it had been, when there was a serious shortage of basic necessities. Everything was under glass or on the shelving behind the counters, well guarded by the assistants. No one could get their thieving hands on the torch batteries, plastic funnels, padlocks or the chocolate biscuits – especially the chocolate biscuits – which cost an average Mongolian a week's pay.

Everything was imported. There was some tinned food but not much variety. Entire counters were devoted to the same item. The second and third floors displayed the same wares as the first floor.

A cashier sat in a tiny booth high above the hoi polloi from where she, the exalted one, oversaw all – like Rapunzel in her tower. The staff all wore large, white, unironed, old-fashioned maid's caps that covered their entire heads.

You had to go through a complicated rigmarole before you could buy something. The help, who were behind the counters, told you the price of whatever it was you wanted to buy. Next you went to the cashier and paid. Rapunzel handed you a ticket, and you could then claim the goods. As you could only buy one item at a time, shopping took forever.

A few days later I returned to the department store and persevered until I was served. In forty-five minutes, I managed to buy a tin of pineapple for two dollars. At first I couldn't find anyone to serve me, the staff were all too busy weighing empty cardboard boxes – possibly their main source of revenue – or chatting to each other. Then I couldn't find Rapunzel. She had disappeared and all transactions had ground to a halt. I went to another floor where tins of pineapple were also on the shelves, as they were in at least five other places. There was no other canned fruit, but there must have been an almighty cargo of pineapple. An assistant finally wrote the price on a scrap of paper for me. I took it to the cashier, paid and eventually got my purchase and took off. The assistant chased me around the shop to get the receipt back. Apparently I was not allowed to keep it, although I would have thought that was the very point of a receipt.

In one corner a pharmacy counter was manned by women wearing white coats and strange gauze contraptions on their heads. These outfits were supposed to convince customers that the assistants were some form of medical help and therefore had the authority to prescribe and sell pills and potions. I remained sceptical.

On the top floor a few household goods were proudly exhibited for people to marvel at. A pre-historic television set had a price tag on it that left me speechless. Anything halfway decent or different was difficult to see because, despite the cathedral-wide aisles, immense crowds of gawking, goggling sight-seers blocked the counters. No one was buying, they had just come in to get warm and look at luxuries they could never afford.

One small counter featured a few pieces of jewellery and everyone pushed and shoved to crowd on top of it and gaze in wonder. I'm not a pusher so I got elbowed out. The jewellery, badly displayed under scratched glass-topped counters, was stuck on old bits of cardboard. The prices had been crudely hand-written. It looked like a bunch of kids had been playing shop. Imitation jewellery was very expensive, and the few good pieces of gold looked rough and contained stones that looked like glass. This was the only place in Mongolia where you could buy an engagement ring. I wanted to buy something – not an engagement ring – but could not get served, so I gave up.

The food in our flop house hotel was worse than the food at the camp. The first night the mutton was decidedly tough and gristly. It reappeared at lunch the next day, having mutated from stew to potato pie, but we recognised it. I don't mind eating recycled food, but this was awful. The potato soup was good though.

We walked into town – myself under sufferance. I don't go shank's pony willingly, but I was press-ganged into it. It was a five-kilometre hike and the wind was glacial, straight off the polar cap. There was still some ice and snow on the nearby mountain tops, but the sun shone, and it was a beautiful day.

We investigated the small shops. There were only a few, and they looked the same as other buildings, with small wooden doors that opened directly onto the street and had no display windows. BB had told us to look for people going in and out of a building to identify a shop. This resulted in my visiting some peculiar places. The shops consisted of a small, cement-floored room divided in two by a glass-topped wooden counter, which you had to bend over to see the goods secreted below. In food shops, we saw such delicacies as goats' ears, black sausage and chicken feet. All lay on top of the counter in open tin trays.

The shops and the goods varied little, some having only half a dozen items for sale. We found a couple of clothing shops where garments, flung over wire hangers, were placed behind the counter and well out of reach – there would be no playing with the merchandise. I could see why the Mongolians shopped at these small places. I bought the same locally made leather gloves that cost one million *togrogs* in the department store for one thousand here. But the prices in the two souvenir and art shops were higher than in the department store despite all these shops being government owned. There was no reason to the pricing, which varied enormously.

While exploring the area around our apartment I found a 'shop', comprising a couple of shelves in the ground-floor apartment in the building next to our hotel. Here a large bottle of vodka cost one thousand *togrogs* compared to eight thousand at the department store. A postcard cost two *togrogs*. I had previously bought some from the UB hotel for four hundred and fifty!

The pharmacies, or *apotiks*, as they were called, were interesting. Name it, pay the price and you could have it – antibiotics, analgesics, the lot. A teller sat behind a glass-screened counter, like in a bank, and glass cases on the counter displayed items for sale – Garamycin, unwrapped condoms, baby teats, and so on. Everything was expensive. You could buy one pill or twenty.

There was one book shop, but most people seemed to buy their books second-hand from vendors who set up shop on trestles on the footpath, or stacked books along the tops of walls in the street. They did a good trade and had books in many languages, especially English. Denise bought a delightful old edition of Mongolian fairy stories for a few cents, and I bought a book of Mongolian poetry. I fondly imagined its contents would lean heavily to horses and romance, but instead the poetry was driven by a revolutionary fervour to revolt against oppression by the landlord class.

The city of Ulaan Baatar is three hundred and fifty-years old. Sixty years ago it was a small town almost entirely made up of felt *gers*, but it now covers an area of 136,000 hectares and has a population of 548,000, seventy per cent of whom are under thirty-five. The birth rate is high, but life expectancy is only sixty to sixty-four years. Consequently Mongols, with their frost-bitten red cheeks and cheery clothes, appear youthful. Most have dark skin, which originates, along with the red cheeks, from exposure to cold air, and wider and flatter faces than the Chinese.

Most people wore the traditional unisex *del*, a long, loose robe trimmed with brocade. The garment was cut in one piece, including the sleeves and high collar, over-lapped widely in the front and was tied with a waist-band called a *bus*. The *del* was secured by buttons of silver, agate or other stones, or cloth tied in knots. Bright coloured *dels* – blue, claret and green – were worn on holidays; darker colours were worn on normal days. Sometimes the *dels* were covered in silk or brocade and looked like fancy dressing gowns and in winter they were lined with sheep-skin or cotton wool. Each ethnic group had its own *del* style. Women wore the *del* like a dress, long enough to cover their high boots. The waist-band sash acted as a soft corset to protect the back when riding long distances, and men attached their sheathed knife, snuff bottle or tobacco pouch to it. The pipe was tucked in their *mongol gutal*, or boots, which were made of thick, unbending leather without heels and with pointed, upturned toes – to prevent kicking the soil and 'disturbing the earth's blessed sleep', as well as to stop the stirrups slipping off. Everyone wore boots in Mongolia, but the women wore softer ones than the men.

The national headgear, the *janjin*, also worn by both men and women, was a hat for all seasons. It had a distinctive round shape, an upturned, scalloped brim, sometimes trimmed with fox fur, and a pointed top that peaked in a knot. In the 1930s men had adopted western-style hats and many men still wore them with traditional dress, making them look like left-overs from Humphrey Bogart films. I noticed that some men sported moustaches, which were rare in China.

On 11 and 12 July, Mongolia comes to a halt to celebrate the summer holiday of *Eriyn Gurvan Naadam*, which translates as Three Men's Games. Despite the name, more than three men, many children and even some women, play at wrestling, archery and horse racing. Women shoot in archery competitions and ride, but they don't wrestle. Children race on horses – they learn to ride before they can walk – over thirty kilometres. This had been the distance between the staging posts that were the only means of transport and communication until the 1920s. The winner gets *khoumis*, the loser a song, and for the very last, who is called the Full Stomach, there is a special song.

The central district of Ulaan Baatar surrounds Sukh Baatar Square. In the middle of this immense square is the mausoleum and monument to the leader Sukh Baatar, who led the revolutionary struggle of the 1920s. He was, of course, mounted on a splendid horse.

The Palace of Culture – where the Central Committee of the Mongolian People's Revolutionary Party meet – is also in the square, as is the National Museum. The State Opera and Ballet Theatre, an impressive red building fronted by white columns, stood out, blooming like a flower among weeds, in the surrounding grim Soviet architecture. The city has an industrial area located in the suburbs. Most of the industry was developed by the Russians in an effort to modernise the country.

On our second day, the heat was turned on. Heat was government controlled throughout Ulaan Baatar, even in hotels and apartments. It was not usually let loose until 15 October. Maybe they had relented because it had snowed or, more likely, some high official was chilly. It was wonderful to thaw out and be warm again.

By the next morning my life was complete. I was happy, warm and fed, and I had slept. I was even about to have clean undies – my washing was drying on the iron heater pipes. I had plugged the kitchen sink by stuffing a face washer in the hole, and had done my smalls. Before I had gone to bed I had turned the mattress over and got rid of the bumps, made another pillow by stuffing the pillow case with some soft clothes, and removed the light bulb from its socket. People could then turn it on all they liked. I didn't care if they fell over in the dark, as long as they did it quietly.

That morning we were taken to see the Museum of Fine Arts, which had an excellent collection of *tankas*, or embroidered collages, paintings on scrolls and Tibetan-style Buddhist statues. *Tankas* were brought to Mongolia with Buddhism and were originally used as religious icons. Their intricate composition flowed in elegant lines of pure, natural colours. One mammoth modern *tanka* had taken nine women three months to sew and appliqué.

Mongols believe all that is beautiful has its origin in nature. Even the poorest, nomadic cattle breeders had richly ornamented clothes and jewellery and carried a traditional cup made from a hollowed tree root and set in chased and decorated silver. Every household item was a decorative work of art – knives, flints, stirrups, horse gear, furniture, garments and boots.

After these delights it was on to the Winter Palace – the real one – a wooden temple, pavilion, and palace. It was once the home of the last Mongolian king, Bogdo Gegen (1869–1924). I went to gaze dutifully at the great beds and thrones and fancy, floor-length robes of richly embroidered brocade and silver-trimmed silk that were lined with fabulous furs.

After lunch the Dirty Dozen had me walking again. I resisted, but there were twelve of them and only one of me. The weather was warmer now and I was down to wearing only three layers of clothes topped by a cardigan, and looked merely fat, rather than pneumatic. It was still too cold for the snow to melt, and it remained on the ground in the lee of our building and on the sides of the mountains. The group set a cracking pace all the way to town with me protesting in the rear. They were a nice bunch of people, but they had absolutely no idea how to take a couch potato stroll. Belting along like marathon walkers, they took huge strides with their great long legs, while I ran behind panting and whingeing. As I hiked along, I passed dismal-looking women selling single cigarettes. They squatted on the pavement and held an open packet out invitingly to passers-by.

By the time we reached the city I wanted a Bex and a good lie down, but I settled instead for the civilisation of the UB Hotel foyer. Denise and I installed ourselves in a spot where the sun came cheerfully through the big window and fell on our comfortable leather couches. We met an Australian woman who had just spent a month in Mongolia on a hunting trip with her husband and his friend. They had fried out in the Gobi desert, frozen in waist-high snow in the north, and been bogged in mud up in the mountains. They had lived in gers, eaten smelly local food and been sick. The trio had equipped themselves with guides, interpreters and terrible drivers, most of whom had nearly killed them by screaming down mountains in their hired jeep. The

167

vehicle, although only a few months old, was a wreck held together with fencing wire. The woman said she had had an awful time, but that they had bagged a lot of game: ibex, big-horned wild sheep, and other animals. I thought that their troubles served them right. The animals got some revenge.

I also met Omar, an Egyptian businessman who was giving the locals instruction in the leather trade. This seemed to entail spending a great deal of the day eating two-hour meals with masses of drinks in the company of groups of Mongolians.

Omar was staying at the other supposedly upmarket hotel in Ulaan Baatar. He said that the food there was terrible and expensive, and that there was no hot water. Most people who could ate at the UB, as we did whenever possible. It was the only place in town that had half-way decent grub, even if it was strange at times. It was certainly cheap. But the hotel guests said that the hot water supply was haphazard and that it took half an hour to get through the pipes.

The Mongolians had a prodigious propensity for alcohol. Boozing seemed to be the national sport. I watched in wonder as four businessmen having lunch drank a big bottle of vodka and a dozen or so cans of beer and still managed to walk out steadily. I was told that the city streets were dangerous after dark, not only because theft was common, but because of drunks. It was particularly unsafe for men who might be mistaken for Russians.

Omar insisted on joining us in the UB dining room for lunch and wanted me to meet him for dinner that night. His face fell when I said I would have to bring my friend as we were advised not to go out alone.

One evening we went to a cultural performance in the beautiful Opera and Drama House. The orchestra comprised a flute, two *morin khur* – banjo-like traditional Mongolian instruments that have long handles with horses' heads carved on them – and a table which enclosed in its fretworked sides a set of strings that the operator hit with two paddles. A hybrid of a piano and a xylophone, it produced a strange, but not unpleasant, sound. The singing, however, was a bit of a worry – a cross between a yodel and a shriek. A female contortionist performed some horribly unnatural moves, which probably did her a lot of harm and didn't do much for me either. She was followed by several horse dances which were wild and frantic with Red Indian war whoops and much Cossack kicking. The costumes were gorgeous: long, brightly coloured silk brocade robes that reached almost to the floor and were tied by sashes or belts, and soft tip-tilted boots. One dressed-up version of the national outfit had high, puffed sleeves that looked as though there were bicycle seats stuck up them, and long strings of beads that hung either side of the face from an elaborate head dress.

The concert was conducted in the Mongolian language, which sounded like an agreeable cross between Arabic and Russian. It was not as harsh on the western ear as Chinese – the dialect around Beijing sounding especially brutal to us.

One day Denise and I called into the UB for afternoon tea. Finding nothing left, I ordered a chicken salad. It came in a small cocktail glass with a tiny fork. Ordering from the menu with its fractured English was like a lucky dip. My coffee, which by local economy standards was expensive at seventy cents, came combined with sugar and milk, there was no separating them. Coke came in cans half the normal size and cost one dollar thirty, but a big pot of tea was a ridiculous seven cents. The menu offered a local wine called *muckta*. No thanks. I'd had enough of local wines after the Chinese effort and the name seemed to spell out a warning.

Next day the taps in our cell block bathroom produced some hot water, which made the day special. The omnipresent thermos of hot water was always available, but the young woman in charge of the cell block looked at me as if I was deranged when I asked for cold water to drink. Why would I want cold water when I could have hot?

It was another dazzling, sunny but cold morning as we set off in the crystal clear air for yet another gallop into town. Outside our building an old woman wearing woollen gloves picked up litter and put it into a hessian wheat bag. The wide streets were swept clean by workers wielding witches' brooms made from bundles of sticks. The sweepings were collected by hand, put in large iron drums and burned on site. There was little traffic and only a few traffic lights. Cars usually stopped at the lights, but buses didn't, and there was still the danger that cars would come roaring around corners. Drivers also had the habit of turning in the middle of the road and coming at you from the wrong direction. Despite these perils, horsemen would ride, with no apparent concern, through the traffic or along the footpaths of the main streets. Everyone gave way. The horse still ruled in Mongolia.

Anton, the charming Frenchman who said he wanted to go to Australia because he wanted to go 'to ze bitch' (beach), guided us, map in hand, to the Choijin Monastery and Museum of Religion. Built in 1908 for holy man Luvsanhaidavt, the brother of one of the Mongolian khans, it was deserted, even though it was in the main part of the city. We entered via the impressive, carved wooden gates found at all important sites in Ulaan Baatar and were stung with an inflated 'special tourist' price. It took one American dollar to broach the gates, but they had forgotten to jack up the price of the substantial book on the history of the place, which was a real bargain at fifty cents.

The monastery grounds were overgrown and unkempt, and long grass grew on the roofs of the buildings, but the complex retained a quiet charm, and it was easy to imagine its former loveliness. Inside the temple the old woman attendant took a stout pole and poked open the wooden shutters covering the fretwork screened windows. I could see that the temple was packed with statues of the Buddha. Brass, wood, gilded, and painted in different sizes, the statues were stacked from floor to ceiling. Some were in glass cabinets that had carved and painted wooden frames.

The central place of honour in the main temple was occupied by a large gilded statue of the Lord Buddha sitting on an elaborate golden throne surrounded by lesser statues and accompanied by demons and other fine fellows. Offerings of Mongolian bank notes had been lain before the statues or placed in their hands, one thousand *togrog* notes taking pride of place. This temple, crammed with god after god, Buddha upon Buddha, emanated an overpowering feeling of religion. The walls were covered with large pictures of heaven and hell, the latter depicting graphic, gory illustrations of the tortures awaiting sinners, which were guaranteed to keep you on the straight and narrow. They showed evil doers being devoured by wild animals, dissected by demons, or decomposing in frozen caves. The hell of Mongolia had a lot to do with freezing, as opposed to the burning of warmer climates – cold was seen as a punishment, whereas in hot countries the villains got scorched.

I bought an old sepia photograph, mounted on a 1920s Russian photographer's card, of the gentleman who used to live in the temple, and then left the group to go alone to the Winter Palace. The day before I had found a Mongolian man selling old bits and pieces outside the gate there and he had promised to bring me an antique jade snuff bottle. Leaving the Choijin Monastery I passed several cows calmly eating the grass that grew where the footpaths would have been if the street had run to that sort of thing. Their attendant dog watched me carefully in case I made off with one. Sometimes in Mongolia I felt as though I was visiting another century.

I waved down a taxi. It was in fact the only one I ever found in Ulaan Baatar, where real taxis were rare. The usual way to transport yourself around town was to stand by the side of the road with one arm stuck out and take whatever stopped for you. This was a good way to meet Mongolian men – I saw no women driving cars. But unfortunately the men wouldn't speak to me. Either they were too shy or they didn't like my looks. It was tough even getting a smile from the reserved Mongolians. Except for an occasional shiny Mercedes, most vehicles were decrepit, as were buses and jeeps.

Vehicles here had a hard, short life. I flagged a ride once in an almost new four-wheel drive that had only done six thousand kilometres. Its foot pedals had been mended with rope and its bald tyres were stapled together.

Paying for your ride was no problem. Everyone accepted one hundred *togrogs* per kilometre, and no one ripped you off. You communicated by sticking your fingers in the air to signify one, two, three or whatever.

Although I arrived on time for my appointment, the man with whom I had the assignation did not show up. No one was there except an artist with his pictures propped hopefully against the wall. I guessed that vendors only frequented the palace gates when they heard a tour was coming, and our lot were the only group in town at that time. I managed to convey to the artist what I wanted, and he obligingly went off to get the person with the alleged snuff bottle while I minded his pictures. And subsequently I felt obliged to buy one. It was, of course, a painting of horses, fast trotting through a flurry of snow. I now wake up to see it on the wall in front of me every morning. I call it my jade snuff bottle, because when the snuff bottle eventually arrived it was very ordinary for its asking price and I did not buy it. The snuff bottle owner bore no grudge but walked down to the road with me and got me a ride with a passing motorist. This was how I learned to get around without wearing out my feet.

15 Aged mares' milk

At lunch in the UB I was adequately fed on something called *moussaka*, which it wasn't. It consisted of stodge piled on top of some minced mutton, which oozed a red oily fat onto the plate. But the accompanying fried cabbage was good and the tomatoes were exquisite, tasting like they used to before all the flavour was bred out of them.

There were always many items on the menu that were not available. I once asked for beetroot salad, 'no got', so I ordered borsch, which did arrive, but with no beetroot. I should have known. It was mostly cabbage with lots of orange mutton fat floating on top, but it was edible. I also had 'meat and potatoes' – lots of spuds and a fair amount of mutton – and 'bread pie', a sort of dry, desiccated cake. Beer, except for the imported European brands, wasn't too expensive, but I refrained from drinking it at lunch. I didn't want to be boozed or asleep by two in the afternoon.

Each Mongolian eats an average of eighty-eight kilograms of meat, mostly mutton, each year. Country people eat even more meat, including beef, camel, goat and horse in their diet, as well as dairy products, wild onions and garlic. Fatty boiled mutton was the favourite food, and the smell of mutton fat permeated everything, everywhere you went. No blood was shed when an animal was butchered. A transverse cut was made in the chest and the heart artery severed. The entire sheep was used, even the blood, which in older days was drunk but was now used for sausages.

Some local delicacies were *boortsog*, butter biscuits fried in oil, and *boondag*, a goat or tarbagan carcass that had had the entrails removed through the neck, hot stones inserted and then barbecued. Meat, air-dried in long strips, had constituted the food of the army on the move in the past, and was still part of the staple diet. Mares' milk was drunk neat or added to tea with salt. The tea, pressed into large bricks, was a special variety only available in Central Asia and China. Dried curdled milk, said to be the substance that gives Mongols their healthy teeth, was served as a snack or put into tea – which in my view made the tea even more disgusting, as if the salt was not enough. *Khoumis* was mares' milk that had been put in a leather bag, churned, curdled and aged. It was slightly spritzig and intoxicating, but that's the only way in which it resembled champagne. It could be distilled into vodka, ten to twelve per cent proof alcohol, a redeeming feature that couldn't be claimed for any of the other drinks. *Khoumis* contains vitamins A, C and B and is said to retard the growth of pathogenic micro-organisms, be effective against lung and stomach diseases, brace the nervous system, and improve the appetite and digestion. Hippocrates said that aged mares' milk cured tuberculosis. It certainly braced my nervous system.

Now that I had learned to wave my arm to obtain a ride easily, I gave up walking. My feet were totally worn out. I had no idea how to say where I lived, but I knew it was near Shukov's Museum – another legacy from the Russians – so I would say that and point in the general direction.

On the tenth night, everyone except Denise and I left Mongolia on the train for Russia. Kisses and hugs were exchanged all round as we parted. I had been lucky to travel with such an agreeable group. I pinched the mirror from the French girl's room and my domestic life was complete.

Next day we set off to visit a women's group. Denise had met one of the members at the women's conference in Beijing, and she was considering working as a volunteer with the group. Although we had arranged to meet someone at nine when the office opened, it was empty. At half past a pretty young Mongolian woman dressed in boots, jumper and jeans arrived. The appointed woman never showed, but our new friend offered to take us to the Buddhist women's centre and to visit her family in their *ger*.

To return to our cell block we flagged down a car that had seat covers roughly chopped from a gorgeous red antique carpet, and fine animal pelts wrapped around the gear stick. The young driver was a pro. From my seat in the back I watched in fascinated horror as he roared up to two buses and, without a centimetre to spare, put us between them. I muttered in terror and he grinned with delight. The first reaction I had had from any of the drivers I had picked up.

The next morning Denise and I went to the weekly market where ordinary Mongolians went to buy whatever was available, from food to clothes. Heavy black cloud covered the sky, and the air had that dark bluish look that it gets when it's really cold. And the market was not only early morning but outdoor. In this climate!

The car we had commandeered took us through the town and the outer suburbs, where large herds of sheep and cows wandered. We also passed small shops or bus shelters covered by miniature pagoda roofs with upturned corners. Our transport bumped and humped up a rutted dirt track, squeezing between closely packed parked cars and carts. We finally came to a halt in front of a high wooden fence behind which we found the market.

From ancient times the bazaar, or market, had been the traditional way Mongolians bought goods. Shops were a recent innovation. On Sundays one hundred thousand people passed through this market, which could hold up to eight thousand at a time. We were advised not to go to the market alone, and told that it was frequented by all kinds of criminals. We were also warned that faulty goods were sold here, such as home-made cigarettes filled with sawdust. There was no shade or cover, and most sellers put their goods on the ground and stood, or squatted, beside them. Some simply held out items in their hands, but the most upmarket used old folding metal beds as trestles. There was no shouting or hawking, as vendors just waited, huddled and bundled against the cold, for customers to buy.

There was even a small puppy for sale at this market, but thank heavens this was not where the livestock was. We had already passed the market where animals, live or butchered, were sold. The sight of bloody carcases, piled high on dirty old wooden horse carts, was horrible. I remembered that Mongolia was a high risk area for brucellosis, a disease contracted by handling fresh meat or animal dung. The carts and their grisly loads headed towards the town centre. Were they on the way to the UB for our lunch? It was enough to make you turn vegetarian.

Although I was reasonably protected from the freezing

air, I could feel my head going numb. It felt too cold for rain, but snow looked a distinct possibility, and then some sleet hit my face, reinforcing my hypothesis. I could see why everyone wore a hat, so I bought one for a dollar fifty: a black leather Russian worker's cap. A real Lenin hat. I hoped it would not provoke any anti-Russian feeling.

My attention was caught by a snuff bottle an old man was selling, and I flashed some dollars. After a lot of amicable bargaining, performed while standing compressed in the centre of a circle of bodies three deep, I bought it. Despite the crowd, I did not feel threatened. No one was aggressive, they were just curious, and I had little to interest the pickpockets.

It was still very cold when, on our last morning, we were delivered to the Moscow-Beijing train. There had been hot water in the bathroom that morning – a farewell gesture? We'd had none the day before and heating only sporadically, and then at half power, for the last two days. A long hike down the platform to our carriage, which was the second last, led us past a lengthy line of smiling Mongolian guards.

Three hours away from Beijing the conductor collected the sheets and curtains to be washed. I queried her priorities. What about cleaning the loo? It was absolutely putrid. The flush pedal had been broken when we had boarded the train, and the state of the toilet had progressively worsened as time went by. No attempt had been made to fix the pedal or to sluice it out. The smell of ammonia wafted down the corridor. In our compartment, half a carriage from the source, it was quite pronounced.

At last we were winding our way down through the mountains close to Beijing. I hung out of the window to see the Great Wall humping its way across the top of the mountains like a dinosaur's backbone. The train stopped to cool its brakes after coming through the tunnels, and in a little gully filled with ferns and green plants, I spotted marijuana growing wild. Purple, mauve and white flowering creepers ran alongside the railway line, but scattered among all this loveliness was a continuous stream of disposable polystyrene noodle bowls. Welcome back to China.

16 A night at the opera

Pandemonium reigned in the foyer of the Jing Hua Hotel in Beijing. A large group of Chinese tourists milled around the desk. The men all smoked like trains, puffing out dense clouds of smoke from pungent cigarettes, while their leader was blowing his stack. It seemed there were not enough rooms for them. I worried that I might not get a bed, even though I had reserved one before I left for Mongolia. But the receptionist remembered me and promised to hold a room while I went off to change some money. When I returned, a screaming match was in progress. I waited, refraining from harassing the desk staff as the others continued to do. I got a room. It took forty minutes of standing at the desk pretending to be patient, but it pays to be nice in China if you can manage it. At one stage the receptionist smiled at me and whispered conspiratorially, 'No worry, you get room.' The group leader looked positively miffed by my success, and, I think, made rude comments about me.

Armed with the battle-scarred piece of paper that was my admission ticket, I went upstairs and handed it to the two girls who stood behind the barricade at the entrance to the sixth floor. One girl took the paper, the other, after I had forked over the bond money, gave me a key. The first then handed me a another piece of paper. I added it to the pile I had amassed, being afraid to throw any away as I had no idea what was written on them. There seemed to be little organisation. The receptionists downstairs did not know which rooms were occupied and phoned the floors each time they were asked for accommodation.

My room was still being cleaned and I was told to take myself elsewhere. I went to eat in the strange little restaurant out the front. The smell blowing off the river was awful, just like a sewer, so I chose not to eat outdoors. Indoors, in the decrepit transportable shed that resembled a disused railway carriage, I had a marvellous meal of eggplant, chilli, bean curd, rice and tasty tomatoes for one dollar fifty. A big bottle of beer cost sixty cents and it was very good.

I talked to a young Israeli boy who had been travelling for fourteen months, two months of which he had spent washing dishes at a restaurant in Darwin. He had been quoted a price for a train ticket from Beijing to Moscow by Monkey, but when checking with CITS had found Monkey one hundred and forty-nine American dollars dearer.

I watched three men from the yokel tour group gulp down four bottles of the ghastly Chinese whisky. They became progressively more boisterous the more they drank. Surprisingly, they were able to walk from the restaurant, but they took more bottles away with them and I did not see the outcome of their session.

Some of these rustic innocents were billeted on my floor. Behaving like kids on a picnic, they sat in their rooms with the doors open, yelling, smoking up a storm or standing in the corridor to scream to others further along. At five the next morning I was shocked awake by crashing, door banging and shouting. It wasn't a big row – just my neighbours getting up. All the television sets were blaring. I gave up on sleep and, grumbling, did my washing, taking my bad temper out on my dirty clothes.

The weather was cool and the atmosphere dreary and heavy with smog. Denise and I took a bread box taxi downtown. These tiny yellow vans cost less than regular taxis, only one *yuan* per kilometre. In 1980 there were three taxi companies in Beijing, and you could only get a taxi from a major hotel; now there were two hundred and thirty companies and fourteen hundred taxis.

At the bank I discovered that the National Day holiday celebrations were in full swing and all sources of finance were shut for five days. Days later, when I finally gained admission, they dispensed large sums of money with little fuss on presentation of my Visa card. In Hong Kong it had taken an hour of investigation, phone calls, and much signing of bits of paper. I would have thought that China would have taken even longer.

I wanted to buy some envelopes with horses printed on them from the post office. They were, of course, locked away under glass in a stout cabinet presided over by two assistants. These women did their utmost to convince me that I should have some others from an unlocked case. When I refused, the assistant said to her mate, 'Picky bloody foreign woman,' or words to that effect. A Chinese-speaking English woman waiting behind me spoke to them and kindly translated for me. The keys had gone on holiday with the Keeper of the Keys and would not return for a week.

I like post offices. Despite their differences, they are all comfortably familiar, all involved in the same activity of sending mysterious items to far flung places. Beijing's post office was gigantic. In a spacious gallery big enough to hold a grand ball, I posted home two kilos of printed matter, all of which arrived safely. To send a parcel, I first bought some strong brown wrapping paper from one counter. Next I took it and the goods to be mailed to Customs for inspection. The attendant stamped the paper, and I returned to the original counter where the assistant wrapped the parcel neatly for me – all for fifty cents.

We walked on to the Friendship Store, or rather I ran along behind Denise, telling her that it was like trying to keep up with a galloping giraffe. But I was getting fit chasing her, and with all the walking she and the other back-packers had made me do, and all the stairs I had climbed – the lift at the hotel had broken down so I had been leaping up and down stairs like a gazelle to and from the sixth floor – I was getting mountaineers' legs.

I took my films of Mongolia into the Friendship Store to be developed. This cost half the price that it did at home, but it wasn't all that good – then again, neither is my photography.

The taxi, instead of taking us back to the hotel, took us on an unsolicited 'guided tour' of outer Beijing. In the process the driver ran up a large amount on the meter. He said he got lost. We said, 'Tough toe nails.' There was an altercation, and a crowd gathered round the door of the hotel. We gave him three-quarters of the meter price and left him arguing with the doorman.

I paid forty *yuan* to Mr Fu, the hotel's tour organiser, to see famous Chinese acrobatics I had heard much about. I was told to be in the lobby that night at a quarter-past six. I dutifully turned up mentally prepared for Chinese acrobats. At half-past six Mr Fu's offsider came along and said, 'Who's for the opera?' Looking at me he asked, 'Are you?' 'No,' I replied, 'I'm for the acrobats.' I sat on, and after another half-hour I went upstairs to Mr Fu's office, rousing the offsider from the nap he was enjoying on the bed.

'Yes, yes,' he said, 'there was only one person wanting to go to the acrobats, so we didn't go.'

I snapped, 'I know. I was that person. Why didn't you let me know?'

'No, no. We decide not to go because there was only one person. We can't go with one person.'

'But I was that one person. I would have liked you to have told me.'

'Oh, yes,' he said. End of conversation.

To compensate for the forty *yuan* I had lost, I was taken to the Chinese opera the next night. This effort, which could be a marathon all day and half the night session, had been mercifully cut short for foreign consumption, but it still took three hours. Chinese opera is very different from western opera and can be a cultural shock if you have not done your homework. The audience was predominantly Chinese, and talked loudly all the way through as one explained to the other what was going on.

The opera was called *The White Snake* and its plot was about as convoluted as any western one, requiring massive suspension of disbelief. In essence the story's moral was that mixed marriages don't work, especially if you marry a fairy or a snake.

On the principal day of the National Day Holiday, Denise and I set out for the Forbidden City. The gates to the city were in Tiananmen, the ninety-eight-acre square in the heart of Beijing. We had directions written in Chinese on a piece of paper, but it was almost impossible to get a taxi driver to agree to take us. Because of the holiday, there were even more people on the streets. Bicycles by the million pedalled past, completely obliterating the road. One woman had a watermelon in her bike basket which seemed to obscure her vision almost entirely, and another had two bottles of champagne in front of her and a child on the back. Giant tricycles with trays attached behind them were used for everything, and were also out in force. Sometimes I saw an entire family get on one of these contraptions. Women wheeled Chinese baby carriages – beautiful antique wicker and iron contrivances that were multipurpose and used to carry many things besides babies. I heard of one British girl who had taken her baggage home to England on the Trans Siberian Express in such a carriage. Oblivious to the jostling crowds, two men in Mao suits played Chinese chess at the street edge of the pavement, perched on minute stools, and balancing a large board between them.

We found that the taxi drivers who had refused to take us to the city centre were very wise. The traffic was terrible and our progress slow. Bicycles and baby carriages passed us by. After an hour we had only managed to reach the edge of the square. The driver was daring – going over the white line in the middle of the road right into the oncoming traffic and squeezing between two trucks. We eventually abandoned the taxi and walked the rest of the way.

In the square there were literally millions of people. We could not have picked a worse day. Why did they all have to descend on Tiananmen on the day that I had chosen? To reach the gate of the Forbidden City we had to struggle through the throng. Flowering pot-plants had been arranged in patterns along all the footpath edges in the square. Six hundred gardeners had worked for eleven days to complete the floral displays, which were Mecca to every one with access to a camera. I had never seen so many people or so many photographers. Those not indulging in photographic orgies were eating. I joined the legions of eaters and bought, by accident, two thick slabs of plain cake about a foot long with a great bar of imitation cream between them. It was so unpleasant that I bought a lunchbox filled with fried rice and meat, which I ate with chopsticks while walking along. When I had finished, I put my container, to the amazement of the people around me, in a bin. Many Chinese appear not to have grasped the concept of rubbish bins. I saw people fling down wrappers and food in the street. Although bins were set into the concrete of the footpath here and there, a wave of litter on the ground washed against them. The worst impact on Chinese ecology must have been the advent of the fast food wrapper, especially polystyrene. I was again shocked at the wanton waste of food – sticks of satay were thrown away with half the meat untouched in a country that has known catastrophic famine and poverty.

China, particularly Beijing, has horrendous pollution caused by car fumes and the coal that is burned in factories and homes. It was a shock to the system after the superb clean air in Mongolia. Behind the Forbidden City stood Coal Hill. It was built from the earth excavated from the palace moat and was where the royal coal was stored in the Ming dynasty. A pagoda surrounded by a park of trees graced its top, but through the smog I could only see the fuzzy outline of the pagoda and a smear where the trees were. Simply looking at the thick air and realising that I was putting it in my lungs made me feel sick.

Pushed along by the crowd, we finally entered the Forbidden City, only to be caught up in the seething assembly inside. I forced my way through a rugby scrum towards two railed enclosures which led to a ticket office. People were meant to stand between the bars in an orderly line to wait for tickets. But they did nothing of the kind. Denise backed off in alarm, but I fought my way in. It was very frightening. I had never seen people behave like this, shoving, shouldering, and fighting desperately as though their lives depended on that ticket. I got pushed into the middle and was almost crushed. At one stage I was pushed onto the railing so fiercely that I thought I had broken some ribs. The people were behaving like crazed animals. They waved money at the girl behind the counter and screamed at her. She remained unperturbed, but she was protected in a glass case behind a strong barrier. I failed to grasp what could have excited such furious desperation.

Reaching the ticket seller at last I discovered I had endured all that gruesome body contact for nothing. I was in the wrong queue. Foreigners had to use a special ticket office where they paid thirteen dollars as opposed to the three cent local charge. Once the fee would have been death, which was why it was called the Forbidden City. We had to leave our passports, or a large amount of money, in exchange for a cassette player and a tape. But it did produce the smooth voice of Roger Moore, alias James Bond, explaining the wonders.

We approached the tunnel through the main gate, Tiananmen – the Gate of Heavenly Peace. Built in 1651, and over thirty-three metres high, it is, after the Great Wall, the most famous structure in China. In the past imperial edicts were read from the gate's lofty balcony. On 1 October 1949, Chairman Mao, who now remains nearby in an embalmed state, proclaimed the People's Republic of China from the gate. The huge red gates were decorated with eighty-one studs, nine times nine, which was the number of heaven and the emperor. Once again Denise and I were carried along in a crushing pack of people. We entered the tunnel en masse, and were squashed through to the other side. It was like being put through an orange squeezer. We emerged into an open square. It was spectacular.

The Forbidden City is housed in a seventy-two hectare rectangle. You walk five or six kilometres from the front gate to exit from the back gate. Along the way we passed through palaces, pavilions and courtyards where the Ming and Ching emperors had lived and held audience.

The courtyards between the buildings contained fountains, sundials, huge bronze animals and magnificent pieces of marble. They were paved with seven layers of brick so that no one could tunnel in to get at the emperor. We stopped to admire a ramp of sculptured dragons, which Roger told us was made from one single piece of marble weighing in at two hundred and fifty tons. It had been transported forty-eight kilometres from Farshan county by thousands of labourers, who had dragged it along specially constructed iced roads. We had not gone far when Roger began to flag. Denise said that she didn't think he'd last the distance.

Although we were surrounded by grandeur, it was hard to imagine the sumptuousness of the former inhabitant's lives. I read that the dowager empress, Tsu Hsi, the power behind the throne from 1861 to 1908, had had twenty-eight ladies in waiting, twenty eunuchs, and eight female officials as her personal attendants, and that every day lunch consisted of a hundred and twenty-eight dishes.

I was disappointed that there were no pieces of porcelain or fragile treasures displayed. But there were some superb pieces of jade and cloisonne placed well back in the palaces where you could only peer at them. The walls and ceilings of the pavilions were works of art covered with intricate mosaics in glorious colours and patterns. I saw Khubla Khan's huge jade wine container made in 1265. It had been lost for centuries but found recently doing honourable duty as a pickle jar in an obscure monastery.

Towards the rear of the complex there was a lovely garden, where ancient trees with twisted trunks guarded an artificial mountain. The mountain had a door at the bottom and stairs through its centre to the top, where there was a small pagoda for the sole use of the emperor.

Roger's batteries were failing. We managed, by giving him a bang every now and then, to get him to the last station, but by then he sounded as though he was gargling under water. My feet, like Roger's batteries, had also given out.

Denise had to pick up her luggage from the hotel and catch a plane to Thailand that evening. We discovered that all the taxis waiting at the exit gate of the Forbidden City had broken meters or the price they quoted was ridiculous, so we decided to walk. There seemed to be a million taxis in Beijing, and most of them passed us that afternoon. After walking quite a distance, we finally scored one. The driver turned around and went back along the road we had just trudged over – we had been going the wrong way. But at least now we were sitting down.

As we drove past the Forbidden City, I could see the enormous moat, big enough for the QE2, that ran alongside the city's ancient, crenellated walls. On its banks huddled a line of antiquated stone hovels. One row leaned right against the wall, graphically showing abject poverty embracing extraordinary opulence.

The taxi driver couldn't find our hotel and, after stopping twice to ask directions, he turned off his meter so that we would not be charged for the time he spent finding the hotel. How different from our last experience.

The next day was another public holiday and, feeling I could no longer face the crowds in the streets, I rested and planned my escape from Beijing. I decided to go back to Mongolia, this time to Inner Mongolia. If possible, I would make a pilgrimage to the mausoleum of the Great Khan, Ghenghis, and get to the site of Kubla Khan's – his grandson – legendary city of Zanadu. I asked Mr Fu in the tour office for advice, but he could not help. Information about major train and plane routes was all that was available to him. There seemed to be no communication between the provinces, and asking about an autonomous region such as Inner Mongolia was like requesting a ticket to the moon.

At breakfast I met a pleasant American couple who said that they wanted to leave China as soon as possible. The general consensus among individual travellers – as opposed to tour groups who saw China from a totally different perspective – was that they would not return. On reflection I thought that I would like to come back to visit somewhere special like Tibet, but that was not really China. People get annoyed by the double standards in pricing. I was used to going places where I was charged a bit more because I had more. I think that's fair, but it was different to be exploited as part of blatant official practice. In the end I felt I had come too late, and was disappointed by the pollution, westernisation and desecration of the culture.

Mr Fu told me that it had been announced the day before that the cheapest train fares and all foreigner tickets were going up one hundred per cent. As foreigners were already charged twice the regular amount, this made prices for us ridiculous. The government wanted to discourage large amounts of peasants from using the trains – fewer people, paying more, on the overworked railways was the idea. It would be costly to replace trains so the plan was to conserve them for businessmen and the rich. Mr Fu also told me that the government was trying to discourage individual foreign, especially budget, travellers. They wanted controlled and pre-paid tour groups, whose money went only into the official coffers. The government did not like back-packers. They preferred rich tourists staying at government-owned hotels who would spend a lot of money.

After an hour spent trying to get through by phone to book me a train ticket to Hohot, the capital of Inner Mongolia, Mr Fu gave up and told me how to get to the station by taxi and book it myself. It sounded easy. Go to the station, and go up to the foreigner's booking office on the second floor (which it wasn't, incidentally).

17 Impatient

Getting to the station was one thing, getting into it was another. It had a massive front spread over several hundred yards, which was fenced with iron barricades and contained a seething mass of people. I knew there were entrance gates somewhere, and I could see movement in the mob. I struggled through the crowd, only to discover that I was on the wrong side of the barricade. These obstacle fences were also found down the middle of wide streets to keep the traffic in separate lanes, as well as along some footpaths; you could walk a long way thinking you were on the inside, only to get to the end and find you were on the outside and had to go all the way back and around again.

A large number of people sat or squatted in the station grounds, some sleeping upright against the fences with their belongings around them. These were provincial peasants, their worldly possessions in bundles done up with rope. They had come to the city seeking work or a better life.

There was an enormous number of policemen about. I concluded that half the population of China was employed by the police or army in an effort to prevent the other half from trampling each other to death. It was a nuisance not to be able to simply walk into the station as you could anywhere else in the world, but if free access had been allowed here the place would have been demolished by the impact of so many people.

I battled to the gate in the first lot of barricades. One guard sat perched above the crowd and two others stood either side. The guards stopped people physically, sometimes violently, if they didn't have a ticket to get in. It was Bedlam. After I had been sufficiently buffeted and trampled on, I surfaced in front of the guard and made him understand that I did not have a ticket, but that I desired one madly. He said, I think, 'No, wrong place,' and pointed further on. I could have joined the locals and spat. I went through the same procedure again and this time made it inside. Fortunately, having round eyes and a big nose sometimes works in your favour. Nobody else got either in or out without a ticket.

Inside I approached a ticket seller who dismissed me with a shrug of her shoulders, making no attempt to understand what I wanted. I found another counter where tickets were being sold, but not to foreigners. After bumbling around for half an hour I made it into the main part of the railway station. It was like entering the eye of a cyclone. There were relatively few people and nobody knocked me about.

The station was a fine old-fashioned place but without a great deal of glamour. At the rear end I saw a sign that said 'Information for Tourist'. Under the sign there was a woman selling lollies. She only spoke Chinese and was not interested in helping me.

Undeterred, I stood there until, to get rid of me, she pointed towards the back of the building where I saw a sign that said 'International Waiting Room', another euphemism for 'First Class'. A guard stood by the heavy swinging doors to repel lesser beings.

I entered this vast chamber, a long room with ninety-foot ceilings, rather like a mausoleum. On a side wall in the corner I saw the obscure sign 'International and Foreigners' Office'. This small niche was engulfed in a crowd of people frantically trying to buy tickets. Most of these people were Chinese and I was pushed out of the way from both sides. But by now I was becoming less western – I could use chopsticks with aplomb and drink coffee from a soup bowl without a blush – so I stuck out my razor sharp elbows defiantly, planted my feet firmly on the ground and leaned on the counter. A rocket would not have moved me. The Chinese, undaunted, shoved their arms in front of my face to present their forms.

It took an hour to buy a soft class sleeper ticket on the next day's train to Hohot. Although the cheaper tickets had doubled in price that day, I got mine at the old Chinese rate for soft class – half the amount previously charged to foreigners. The new foreigners' price had not yet been announced, and the seller did not know what to charge me. I hoped it was in fact a ticket for Hohot. I was not sure I had pronounced it correctly, but I would board the train and see what eventuated.

Greatly pleased that I had succeeded at the difficult task of buying a train ticket alone, I was now ready try public transport. If my map hadn't indicated that the subway station was across the street from the railway, I would not have found it. A sign in Chinese and a wall around the steps leading underground made it ambiguous.

Trotting down an enormous flight of stairs, I found a system similar to the one in Hong Kong and on which I could ride anywhere for half a *jiao*, pronounced *mao*, one tenth of a *yuan*. The trains ran frequently but were crowded. When a train pulled in, passengers stampeded towards the doors, surging aboard before people could get off. But for me it was an event. I not only got on the right train, I got off at the right station.

I celebrated my successful morning with lunch in a French cafe named 'Vie On France'. I ordered black coffee and was given a pale brown liquid that the staff insisted was black. I think something was lost in the translation. But the pizza I had was the best I had ever eaten, a scrumptious base covered with great chunks of munchies an inch thick, not the miserable little shavings you usually get. It amused me that I had spent two years in Italy, but had to admit that a French cafe in China made the best pizza I had tasted.

In a nearby supermarket I bought a big jar of dill cucumbers for fifty cents, and joy! I found some cheese. I had been four weeks without any. Although it was available in some tourist shops in China, it was rare and expensive. This was a soft French Camembert and by the time I got it back to my room it was running everywhere and smelled like old socks. But it was delicious.

One of Beijing's wonders was the Temple of Heaven. A perfect example of Ming architecture, it had been built around 1406 in an elegant circular shape with a peaked roof like a Mandarin's cap. It was beautifully decorated outside and could be seen sparkling from a distance like a precious jewel. No nails or fasteners had been used in its construction; it was made entirely by using interlocking wooden pieces. The temple was located in Tiantan Park, six hundred and sixty-seven acres covered with trees, mainly pine and Cyprus, many of which were over five hundred years old. The park was enclosed by a massive old wall. The emperor had come to the temple twice a year to pray for a good harvest, humbly taking upon himself all the sins of the people and asking forgiveness for them.

Entrance to the grounds cost the Chinese a quarter of a *yuan* but I could not pass as one, so I was charged thirty. The park was sprinkled with pagodas and seats, and children's playgrounds. I noticed that no one had more than one child with them.

The temple gardens consisted of flowering pot plants that had been massed together and arranged in various colours to form precise geometric shapes and patterns – red poinsettias, white daisies and dahlias and a mauve flower that resembled love in a mist – that complemented the colours of the temple's exterior.

Outside Tiantan Park, I discovered the Hongqiao Market. Supposedly an antique market, it seemed to have mostly touristy reproductions and rubbish, with only a few genuine antiquated objects. There were also small animals for sale. Two baby monkeys played together, frolicking around in a tiny cage oblivious to their miserable situation, while a small boy poked his finger through the wire trying to hurt them. I hoped they would bite him. I remembered the time I did not get to see the circus because my big sister poked her finger through the monkey cage on our way in and we ended up seeing her get a tetanus needle instead. A large monkey was doing back flips in a cage so small he could only just stand up. I suppose he was longing for a fling in the trees, poor thing. And a small animal like a pygmy possum, imprisoned on a treadmill in the centre of a minute circular bamboo cage, ran continually round and round. This looked like utter torture.

'*Neehow*,' (Hello) a loud voice said in my ear. I turned and found myself facing a large, black bird with a bright yellow bill. This chatty soul amused everyone, especially me. I had not heard a bird speak Chinese before. The Chinese love birds and will pay huge sums for rare ones. Then, too often, they put them in tiny cages or eat them.

Before taking off for Inner Mongolia I succumbed to the urge to improve my hair. It was looking flat and boring, and I thought some colour might brighten it up. I saw some boxes of hair colouring that looked promising. The colours were, understandably, all red and black. I chose dark mahogany thinking that there would be instructions inside the box. There were: they said, 'Leave on twenty minutes because you want black if other colour, steam forty minutes.' I left it on for thirty minutes and came out a flaming scarlet! I never learn.

The next day I packed my bags and left. The taxi dropped me in the street outside the railway station and once again I had a problem broaching this fortress. Luckily I found a spot in the barricade where an enterprising soul had prised one of the rails aside to crawl through. I followed and pushed my bags through to the other side. As my train did not leave until seven in the evening I asked if I could put my bags in one of the storage lockers in the International Waiting Room. The attendant and the guard gave this a lot of thought before, after much sorting of keys and discussion among themselves, they agreed.

With several hours to spare, I went to the Palace Hotel to look at an exhibition of goods to be sold at the forthcoming Christie's antique auction in Hong Kong. The viewing was held in the stupendous Crystal Ballroom, named for its six gigantic chandeliers that glittered and sparkled on each side of the room. The pieces to be auctioned were also stupendous: apple green jade so flawless and perfect it looked like plastic and stunning antique porcelain and paintings. But I learned something. I had not realised that the under-glaze of the earlier pieces of Ming porcelain was the colour of dried blood.

The foyers of top-class Chinese hotels were so big

and so superlative they had to be seen to be believed. A torrential waterfall cascaded down through the centre of the Palace foyer, falling from the third floor to the basement where it mingled with jets of water rising from a fountain below.

The Beijing International Hotel, another extravaganza, was also in the vicinity. Among the masses of expensive shops on the second floor I found a Chinese medicine booth where I bought a potion alleged to combat hay fever symptoms. It cost only two *yuan*. I had no idea what it contained, but it worked.

While in the Beijing I visited their wash house. I never missed an opportunity to sample the loo in a first-class establishment in China. I became a connoisseur. First-class hotel bathrooms were wonderful. They had attendants who rushed up to hand you warm towels. And they had toilet paper! It was bliss! I resisted the urge to put some in my pocket. The attendants do not get tipped but they still smother you with attention. They leap to their feet when you come in to show you where to go. The attendant in the Beijing hotel actually took me around the corner and opened the door of the loo for me.

My guide book said that CITS were located in the Hotel Beijing. I thought I would ask them if I could travel by coastal ship from Tianjin to Shanghai after I returned from Inner Mongolia. I wandered around the hotel looking for their office. A receptionist sent me to the eighteenth floor where, in a maze of dimly lit corridors, I found CITS. The door was locked. I banged on it until it opened. The young man had been having a snooze. He reclined in a chair, shoes off and feet up on the only other chair. He removed one foot from this as a concession to my appearance, but did not make any space for me to sit. He treated me in the manner I came to associate with CITS, not rude, just not interested – as if to say, Why are you bothering me with this, it has nothing to do with me. In limited English this gentleman told me that no boats left from Tianjin. I said, 'Yes they do. They go to Chingdoa.'

'No,' he said. 'No.'

'Then they go somewhere else.'

He reluctantly admitted that they did. So I said, 'Well, then, they go from there to Dalian and from there to Shanghai.'

He finally agreed. But it was torture getting the information out of him.

I wandered back to the train station along a road lined with rows of stalls that sold goods likely to interest travellers. While I was buying some mandarins, a small child came and squatted alongside me. The split in her pants opened conveniently, and she peed on a tree.

The International Waiting Room boasted a coffee house, but it only served biscuits and those deplorable three-in-one packets of coffee, sugar and milk combined. I procured, by the use of a lot of hand signals, some food at the other end of the station where the ordinary people ate. The lad serving there handed me a tray heaped with more food than an army could have got through. I ploughed into it, listening to the scrunching, gnawing noises all around me – a sound I shall always associate with China.

The male guard in the waiting room greeted me like a long lost-friend and helped me retrieve my suitcase. We found my key and released my luggage from bondage. I bought a beer from the coffee house. There were no glasses. It came in a can complete with a straw. I got my mug out of my bag. It is against my religion to drink beer through a straw.

The train left from a platform a long way away and to reach it I had to go upstairs and down again. I tried to use the lift, but no one could find the operator and it was locked. I threw my bags and myself on the only escalator I ever saw working in China. The station was immense, and you had to be able to recognise the Chinese number for your train. *En route* I passed through the hard class waiting room, a nightmare seething with people. I came to a turnstile blocked by several participants in a heated argument. People were always trying to get into places where they were obviously not entitled to be by arguing with guards. By now I knew enough not to stand back and wait politely. I pushed my ticket in front of these people and was let through.

I went further and further until I came to two very long, steep flights of stairs. While I stood contemplating them, two young railway guards came along and carried my bags down for me. At the bottom I had to traverse miles of uneven platform alongside a lengthy train, which was now hooting and sounding ready to go.

At each carriage I showed the guard my ticket, hoping that this one was mine, only to be sent further down the train. I was almost to the end, and in a panic, before I found the correct one. As I heaved my bags up the step under the critical eye of a hatchet-faced conductor, a kind middle-aged woman gave me a hand. She and her husband were sharing a compartment with me and were also *en route* to Hohot. Although the only words we had in common were thank you, this lovely Mongolian couple were incredibly good to me. They helped me stow my luggage, and the wife got the plastic travellers' shoes from under the bed and showed me how to put them on. I didn't want to – they were the standard size, ten times too big for me – but I wore them to make her happy. She noticed that I was bleeding from where I had cut my foot and insisted on putting a band-aid on it. Her husband, meanwhile, was telling me, I think, that if I did not wear the band-aid I would get infected. I thought privately that I would be more exposed to infection if I sealed in the dirt I had picked up around Beijing that day, but she was so sweet and motherly I could not say no to her.

Although they did not make it obvious, my companions wanted to go to bed at eight o'clock, so I clambered up into my bunk and read for a while. I did not sleep well. During the night one of the railway guards came and slept in the bunk opposite me. He kept waking up at frequent intervals to turn the light on and off. All three of my companions snored loudly and when the train stopped every couple of hours the noise was intensified by the station din. Then, as we got further north and climbed into the mountains, I felt the cold starting to creep into the carriage.

The toilet was nowhere near as bad as the one on the Mongolian train had been, but by morning it was decidedly smelly and the floor was awash with urine. I suddenly realised that was why plastic sandals were provided.

Looking at the pile of rubbish that had accumulated in the corridor, I decided that if the Chinese were taught how to use queues and rubbish bins, half of them would be out of work. One half of the population seemed to be employed to clean up after the other, or to prevent them from stampeding each other to death. The Chinese would not stand in line or wait for anything. For example, as I was entering the bedlam of the Beijing railway station entrance, my bag and I were half way through a turnstile only big enough for one when a well-dressed, middle-aged Chinese woman came at me from behind and squeezed in with me, trying to shove me out of the way so she could go through first. I stuck to my guns and refused to be pushed back. She persisted and managed to compress herself into the turnstile with me, struggle through and emerge in front of me. I recognised her later in the waiting room. How could I forget someone I'd been that close to? She sat in there for hours and I wondered what the point had been of her nearly beating me to death to get in the grounds half a second before I did. China was a nation of terribly impatient people.

18 Hard class

I awoke in Inner Mongolia. A line of slate-blue peaked
mountains stood close by the railway line. As the sun rose
it turned the mountain ridges a delicate pink in contrast
to the sapphire, shaded valleys. It was great to breathe
clean fresh air again, even though it was very cold. I felt
as though I was giving my lungs a holiday.

We came to the outskirts of Hohot, which means blue
city, a reference to its skies. The city lies twelve hundred
metres above sea level. Inner Mongolia stretches across
half of northern China and suffers severe winters with
Siberian-style blizzards and raking, cold winds. Tempera-
tures can drop to minus thirty-two-degrees Celsius.
I planned not to be around to find out what that is like.

Inner Mongolia is made up of the southern provinces
of the Mongol homeland. These provinces were taken
over by the Chinese communists in 1947 and declared
an 'autonomous region', which it is not. China rules it.
Since Russia left Outer Mongolia, and since the surge
in Mongolian nationalism, China has tightened its hold
here. China transported large numbers of settlers, mostly
Han Chinese, into Inner Mongolia, but Mongolians

remain Tibetan Buddhists. The country is mostly grass-land, and the economy is based on grazing large numbers of sheep, cattle, camels, and the five million horses the area boasts.

At Hohot station my good-hearted companions not only helped me off the train and assisted me with my luggage, but also made it clear that they would take full responsibility for settling me somewhere. They led me the shorter way out through the back of the station, found someone to carry my bag, got into a bread box taxi with me, and accompanied me to the hotel I had chosen. Then they carried my gear in, helped me register and made sure I was settled in a room before phoning for someone to collect them.

The Hotel Xincheng consisted of several pleasant old buildings set in a park among a flock of grazing sheep. The wing in which I was billeted was two storeys high and had an upstairs balcony all the way across its front. My room was large with very high ceilings. But there was no heating. It was the old story: no heating until the fifteenth of October when all public heating comes on. It was now the tenth, and it was freezing! But the room was a fair imitation of reasonably decent hotel accommoda-tion; it was fairly clean and most of its accoutrements were in passable condition, though not all worked.

I had something to eat and a hot drink. The service was excellent. As soon as I arrived a room attendant brought me tea and hot water. The staff didn't demand key deposit money here. They didn't trust you with a key! Every time I went in or out, I had to ask the little lady who sat and watched the front door from the window in her bedroom wall to lock or unlock the door for me.

It was still only mid-morning so I lay on the bed and tried to read, waiting for the day to warm up. But it got colder instead and even when I crept, book and all, under the doonas, the room felt like an icebox. I went to sleep in disgust. Three hours later I woke up to see the sun coming in the window. When it had warmed the room enough to be tolerated, I crawled out of bed and went for a walk. It was quite pleasant outside in the sun and my down overcoat protected all of me except my face, which was frozen.

I walked the short distance to the Inner Mongolia Hotel, the main hotel in the town, and reputedly the hideout of CITS. I was going to ask them how to get to Dhongseng, the nearest town to the site of the Khan's mausoleum. The enormous hotel had an area the size of a couple of skating rinks, and as shiny and slippery, between the front door and the reception desk. The friendly hotel staff directed me to the CITS office. I got lost in a labyrinth of rooms, but a bell boy dropped what he was doing and showed me the way, smiling! CITS staff were friendly too, but they were not able to help me, and I wondered why I persisted in trying to make them behave like a proper travel agency. I decided to go to Baotou by train and by local bus from there to Dhongseng.

Hohot has a population of half a million, but the Han Chinese outnumber Mongolians. The streets are broad, and there were not very many cars or trucks, but there were a great many bikes in the wide bicycle lanes. Most buildings were functional and plain, and somewhat depressing to look at.

By half-past five the sun had lost its power, and my room, despite the double glazing, felt as if the arctic winds were blowing through it. I drew the heavy curtains together to close out the light and with luck some of the cold, put on more clothes and went back to bed. And stayed there.

My room was graced by a television, but it didn't work.

It could not be plugged in, because there was no plug near it. The same applied to the desk light. There were two sets of plugs on the far wall, an Australian type and a Mongolian one, but there was no way the appliances could be moved over to them. The phone worked, but the numbers I tried all gave me a recorded message. The toilet cistern trickled continuously, and the bath leaked onto the floor. The hot water came through the taps after a long wait, but once I had got the hang of it, it refused to stop and dribbled all night.

I inspected my pillow. It was small, square, flat and solid, and stuffed with what seemed to be fishing sinkers. They were actually rice husks, as my friend Denise had discovered in Outer Mongolia. She told me that she had thought there was a mouse in her room because she kept finding little articles that looked like mouse droppings. Then one day she noticed that they were coming from a hole in her pillow. The turd-pillows were actually quite comfortable once you got used to them, as they folded to the contours of your head and neck.

The bathroom was blessed with a deep old-fashioned tub, the first bath I'd seen in a long time. I luxuriated in very hot water up to my neck, and got blissfully warm before I went to sleep under my two felt-filled doonas. In the morning I took another bath to get me ready to face the day.

I left Hohot the following morning, on another brilliantly sunny but icy day. I couldn't spend all day in the bath or bed. With nowhere warm to stay, I had decided to leave as soon as possible. Hohot was probably not a bad town, just too cold for a tropical flower like me.

At the railway station I made my way to a shed that looked something like a ticket office. I didn't have a clue what to do next, as all the signs were in Chinese or Mongolian. I tried my luck at a hole in the wall that I thought might be a ticket window. The woman behind it was so stunned at my appearance that all she could do was gape at me in amazement. Maybe it was my hairdo. I tried another window, showing the woman the word for Baotou in my book. She eventually sold me a ticket after much giggling. I realised afterwards that this station did not sell foreigner, or soft-seat, tickets, and that I had bought one of the fabled Chinese-price tickets that are supposed to be impossible for foreigners to get. I had no idea when the train departed or even if I had a ticket for Baotou, but I was certainly going somewhere.

I lumbered through a cheerless waiting room, a freak for the assembly to marvel at, to a turnstile that led into the station yard. The guard on it proved impassable. No amount of ticket flashing impressed her enough to let me through, so I asked directions from a policeman. At least, I think he was a policeman. All officials wear uniforms. Whoever he was, he pointed me in the right direction. I was having trouble hauling my bag along the rough cobblestones, and a man came and offered to help me. I thought he was soliciting a porter's fee, but he didn't ask me for money, so I still don't know who he was. We travelled miles over tracks, paths and railway lines and along several platforms before he deposited me on one. He left, saying he would return and help me again later, which he did.

The train arrived from Beijing. It was *en route* to Lanzhou on a line that cut a long loop through Inner Mongolia. After Baotou, the line heads out to the wild west where trains are often delayed by yaks and sand-storms. My friend/porter and I trundled down the long line of the train until I was permitted to clamber aboard. I realised that my ticket only gained me admission to a hard-class carriage with no seat.

So this was the infamous 'hard seat' I had heard so

much about. It was horrendous! The carriage was full of smoke and packed to the ceiling with people. I figured 'hard' meant not only the state of the seat but the difficulty of getting one. I decided I would prefer something else.

My porter pushed me into the next hard-seat compartment where the first two seats had been made into a makeshift office by the simple addition of a waist-high board between them. Two gents, who apparently had some connection with the railway, were upgrading, downgrading and selling tickets. After much shouting between them, my helper, and everyone else in the carriage who could get close enough to add their bit, I was upgraded. I was given another ticket in exchange for fifty *yuan* and shunted through several carriages into a hard-class sleeper containing six men, one of whom was unceremoniously ejected to accommodate me. It was not far enough to Baotou to warrant anything more than a seat and I said so, but was given to understand that there wasn't one. I shut up and sat down.

My seat was a bunk, one of six that were lined three in a row on either side of a narrow compartment with no door. The contingent in the carriage was entirely male and quite friendly. There seemed to be no hard feelings about my intrusion; they even tried to talk to me. Before long two more men came and sat beside me. Hard-class carriages were too crowded to let a bit of good space go wanting. One of the guards persisted good-naturedly in trying to ask me something. I got out my phrase book and discovered he was asking me how much my watch cost. I wasn't sure if he wanted to swap it or buy it. When I told him it was a cheap Hong Kong watch, his interest evaporated and he went into the toilet at the end of the carriage. When he came out he casually wiped his hands on the window curtains. At least he washed his hands.

It took three hours to travel from Hohot to Baotou. The countryside was agricultural all the way, interspersed with unattractive villages full of grey and brown brick and tile buildings. There were fields between the mountains and the train line that were either brown with ploughed soil lying fallow, or covered with ripe, rippling barley and wheat. Every now and then there were little plots of vegetables and crops of lentils. Poplar trees surrounded the fields or gathered behind them in stands. Some fields were full of peasants reaping the harvest with scythes, threshing with a hand-operated machine, or using donkeys and carts to haul the bagged grain away.

It took a long time to get past the outskirts of Baotou. We went through large industrial areas with huge smoke stacks and mud-brick houses and buildings. The town dated back to the fifth century AD, and was now the biggest industrial centre of Inner Mongolia, not that this was any recommendation. It was extremely ugly.

19 In search of the Great Khan

At Baotou station I arranged to leave my biggest bag in the luggage room in the tender care of the Chinese railways. I found the nearby bus station, and a young man asked me where I wanted to go. I told him Dhongsheng. Before I could stop him, he grabbed my remaining bag and shot off across a courtyard and into the bus depot. I cantered after him. The depot was spacious and almost empty which, after China, made it seem a pleasant building.

I had already decided that I far preferred Mongolia, Inner or Outer, to China. Neither was packed solid with people, and I realised I needed open spaces. I do not tolerate crowds well.

The young man was joined by two others and they hustled me onto a bus. I got one foot up on the step, took a look in, and baulked. This was not the way I wanted to go. The bus was a ramshackle vehicle that was packed to capacity with people and smoke. There were no seats; even the aisle was full. I was not going to travel for several hours standing up. 'No thanks,' I said, and backed off. I tried to get my feet back on the ground while the men did their utmost to push me in. 'No thanks,' I repeated. 'I want a seat.' I patted the back of the seat nearest me. 'One of these.'

They assured me I would get a seat. They man-handled me back onto the bus and showed me a seat they had somehow cleared. It was next to the driver. 'Not for me, mate,' I uttered resolutely. 'That's the suicide seat.' They got the message, and I fought my way off.

A few minutes later, the young men showed me another bus, a small empty one. I chose a seat, settled in, then attempted to buy a bottle of water from an elderly woman who was hawking drinks. I put my hand in my pocket to get my purse. It was gone! I had always said that this would never happen to me. But when I had paid the fee for my luggage storage, I had thoughtlessly slipped my purse into my coat pocket. I had never done that before, but there was no one around, and I did not think for a minute that I was in a situation where I would be robbed. The annoying thing was that I knew it was my fault. I had broken a cardinal travelling rule: never put a purse in your pocket. The water seller commiserated with me, but I had no hope of reporting my loss. No one spoke English and there seemed to be no one in charge of the station.

The bus had to fill with passengers before it could leave. I staked a claim on the seat by putting my coat on it and, enlisting the water seller to guard the coat, went back into the bus station to go to the loo. No one understood me when I asked where it was. I saw a sign above a doorway that looked hopeful. Seated at a table beside it was an old crone who held up two fingers intimating that I wasn't getting in without paying two something. The hell I wasn't. I was in no mood to brook interference. My real money was in my travel wallet, which was secreted on my body, and I needed privacy to extract it. I'm not a complete fool. The pickpocket had only taken my small money, about twenty dollars.

I sailed through the door, ignoring the ancient one's protests, and discovered to my horror that inside was a public toilet. When they said public toilets here, they meant it! An elevated bench, with pairs of foot blocks on it, ran the length of the room. You stepped up and, placing your feet on the blocks, balanced in a squatting position over an open drain. Water ran continuously from one end of the drain to the other, and then out into the street or the river. This set-up allowed you to watch your neighbour's bodily juices slowly drifting past. Several women were already *in situ*. I was too desperate to wait for a secluded spot, so I had to take up a position right in the middle. The others all unashamedly watched me, open mouthed and goggling. Two women finished but, unable to leave the entertainment, came and stood directly in front of me. They discussed me loudly with much hilarity, and gave a running commentary to those without such a good view. In remote villages in Indonesia crowds had gathered outside primitive toilets to watch me by peeking through the cracks of the door, but this was the first time I had ever performed in public.

On my way out I was vociferously accosted by the crone. She was not going to let me get away without paying. She wanted two *fan*, two tenths of a *jiao*, which was infinitesimal. But the smallest note I had now was fifty *yuan*, and she could not give me change.

After waiting a long time while the driver and his helpers did a lot of shouting, beeping, engine revving and shoving people into the bus, we moved off. Luggage was piled high down the centre of the mini-bus. Two people had come aboard with hessian bags as big as wool bales and squeezed them down the aisle so that I could no longer see the driver. Anyone wanting to get in or out had to climb over the bags.

The bus crept through the town, the conductor all the while collecting passengers from the curbs and squeezing them into our midst, until at last we were on the open road. Then he got up on top of the load in the aisle and, tucking his old leather money bag under his head for a pillow, had a nap.

Soon we crossed a long bridge spanning the Yellow River at its northern-most reaches. I could see how it got its name; the water was indeed yellow. The bridge continued for many kilometres along the river, crossing the dry flood plains. After that we drove on a road elevated above vegetable gardens planted on land that also looked as though it was flooded at times. The bus climbed up into steep hills heavily scored by water erosion and winter run off; deep crevices and channels, coloured in multi-shaded layers of dusky pinks and creamy whites, had been formed as the moisture weaved its way downward. We crossed many dry, deep watercourses that I could see only needed the snow and rain to become raging torrents once again. Looking down, I could see how picturesque these mountains were. Their tops were rounded and smooth and bare of foliage except for something that from a distance looked like moss. Mini-grand canyons flowed among them, one folding into another in harmonious patterns.

After we had passed through the mountains we drove among fields where numerous peasants were harvesting. At each village we dropped off and picked up passengers. My neighbour, a good-looking girl of Mongolian appearance, went to sleep on my shoulder. As we got further out the grasslands began and there were a great many animals – donkeys, cows, sheep, goats and horses – in proportion to the few houses. The land rose in low hills covered with clumpy vegetation that looked like saltbush.

The sides of the road were lined all the way by double lines of poplars – planted as part of the government's grand scale re-afforestation plan. Tree freak that I am, this made me happy.

We also drove through an area of sand dune country – the Gobi Desert starts just south of Baotou – where beautiful golden mounds rose and fell away, one lovely high rolling slope after another. After four and a half hours, we came to the centre of a town. A sign in English confirmed it to be Dhongseng. I was relieved to have been on the right bus after all! I could have been anywhere with my knowledge of the language.

I had read that this was a small town, and as far as facilities went it was, but by Australian country town standards it was enormous. Dhongseng's outer suburbs consisted of extensive *ger* settlements, now and then interspersed with larger *gers* that looked as though they were used as storage sheds and municipal offices. Many of the brick or mud-brick buildings were also shaped like *gers*. The main part of the town was a square. It had only a couple of wide streets, and the shops and businesses that lined them were flat-roofed and shabby. Many people were doing business on the footpaths and by the side of the roads – welding, sawing wood, sharpening knives, selling bits and pieces, drying beans, washing clothes and repairing vehicles. Women sat in front of their shops and stalls on stools or chairs, or cross-legged on the pavement. Almost all of them were knitting to get ready for the hard winter to come.

I scrambled down into the muddy yard at the back of the bus station and was immediately grabbed by a man who I thought was offering me a taxi. I later discovered that there was no such thing in Dhongsheng. What I was offered instead was a three-wheeled bicycle with a tin tray on the back. A bicycle ute! I got into the tray, much to the amusement of the passers-by, and was pedalled up one main street and down the other. I had thought, fool-ishly, that the rider knew where to take me, but after a while he stopped at a factory that made cushions. He was determined I should go in there. I dutifully did so and an agreeable man explained to me in English that this was not a hotel but there was one a few doors down. I found the alleged hotel, which looked just like the cushion factory.

Inside the two girls behind the desk insisted that they did not have a room. I smiled a lot and tried to look harmless. With the help of my phrase book I made them understand that I wanted to stay there for the night at least. No price could be elicited from them. I figured it couldn't be too much, even though the room they finally let me see had its own bathroom. They installed me in the room and pointed to 'wait a minute' in the phrase book. I settled myself.

A knock at the door followed soon after. One of the girls beckoned for me to follow her and at the desk I met an older lady who asked me for money. She seemed to be signalling twenty-three *yuan*. I thought I must be mis-taken as that was only just over three dollars, but that was right. None of the foreigners' forms I'd become used to filling in at hotels were produced. I lived in dread that the police would come and throw me out.

There was no hot water in my bathroom, but as usual there was a plentiful supply in the ubiquitous thermos. It was too darn cold to worry about washing anyway, but at least it was not as cold as Hohot. I was now further south and out of the mountains. I was amused that, except for its hot water, my room mirrored the one I had stayed in the night before in Hohot – two floral armchairs, two beds, and two warm doonas – but the cost was under four dollars instead of over forty. What a difference it made to get a hotel at local prices.

The double-glazed windows in my room had a gap where one of the outer windows did not shut properly. I stuffed the crack with spare pillows to keep the cold air out. The window was covered by a tatty cotton curtain that was pulled along a piece of bent wire on safety pins. There was a heater, but it was not the fifteenth of October yet, so it didn't work.

In the bathroom there was a hand basin and a shower that was turned on by a metal lever sticking out of one of the pipes. The loo had an archaic cistern, which didn't work but came complete with a couple of spanners for DIY running repairs. There were enough pipes going through the bathroom for the engine room of the *Queen Mary*. I was afraid of causing a flood if I interfered with these complicated works, so for once I left the plumbing alone. I used a plastic bucket to flush the loo. The bathroom was supplied with all sorts of mops, buckets and brushes. I used one to dry the floor but it was soon wet again from all the leaks.

The light was again only two-candle power. I rigged up my portable lighting kit and then, muffling myself against the cold, set off to explore the street. As I appeared on the steps of the hotel, two men were passing by. At the sight of me they grabbed each other and screamed, laughing, shrieking and jumping up and down. Oh nice, I thought, what a lovely start this is. It did nothing for my confidence as I set off to see the town. Fortunately no one else reacted in this way, but I got a lot of stares and a couple of cries of '*loalas*' (foreigner). Even though I was a sideshow I felt safe in this town.

I was gazing about in the main street when a man popped out of a doorway. I think he asked me if I wanted a hotel. He waved his hand upstairs. I declined. Who knew what he was offering? He then made signs indicating food, and that got my attention. Food is not something any sensible traveller knocks back. You never know when the next lot is going to come along. He led me into a simple room furnished with a couple of rough tables and chairs. Two more men joined him in his efforts to find out what I wanted to eat. This consisted of the three of them standing very close to me, staring intently into my face and shouting at me in Mongolian. The one directly in front of me solemnly picked his nose with a dirty finger. I sincerely hoped he wasn't the cook. I indicated that I would eat anything going. The first man produced an egg for my inspection. I nodded my head eagerly.

After enough time had passed to whip up a forty-course banquet I was proudly presented with a flat, salty, dry and burnt omelette. It was like trying to pull rubber apart with chopsticks, but I struggled on and ate it all. The cook enquired about the next course. I asked for 'jiaozi' (dumplings). He showed me one and I agreed. I thought it was one of those I'd had before that were filled with yummy goodies. It was not. It was just solid plain tasteless dough. At least the cook brought me a large bottle of beer. I never saw a small bottle of beer in China or Mongolia, but it was not as strong as our beer. It was forty-five cents a bottle for the local brew. The most expensive kind was Chingdoa, but it was all good. I felt I deserved it after the day I had been through – rough riding on a local bus, being robbed *and* publicly ridiculed, both in a toilet and outside my hotel.

It was dark when I walked back to the hotel. On the pavements vendors roasted sweet potatoes, chestnuts and other delectables on portable cookers made from forty-four gallon drums. They cut the drum lengthwise, put hot coals inside, a piece of tin on top to cook on, stuck it on a barrow to wheel down the street then set up in business. There were also tiny portable shops on the same sort of barrow but with a couple of rows of shelves for the goods. And portable restaurants. Pieces of canvas or plastic were tied between trees or posts to make walls on three sides and inside them were a couple of small wooden benches, a low table and a brazier to cook on. What more do you need to dine *al fresco*?

Groups of men were playing billiards outdoors on the footpaths. You saw billiard tables on the streets even in small towns in Inner Mongolia, and they were always well patronised. At one of the portable shops I was thrilled to find a jar of what I thought was coffee. The label looked like Nescafé might be written in Chinese. But I was soon horribly disillusioned. I wonder what that label did say. It turned out to be a foul abomination of tea, coffee and sugar mixed together. And I had an enormous jar of it. I had nothing else to drink and as the maxim, 'Waste not, want not', had been thoroughly instilled in me at an early age, I struggled to ingest the rotten stuff.

I was just drifting off to sleep when a terrible commotion broke out in the corridor of the hotel. Doors were being opened one after the other, and banged shut as hard as possible, and there was lots of shouting. To my apprehensive ears it sounded like the Gestapo turning everybody out. The noise approached my door. Someone thumped loudly on it. I heard a key turn in the lock, a man entered, turned on the light, shouted something at me and slammed out again. I lay there terrified, wondering what was going to happen next. Nothing did. Maybe the staff were checking the door to see if it worked, or the hotel manager had forgotten how many guests he had, and had decided to do a bed count. But I think it was a police raid and I'm glad it wasn't me they were looking for. I was pretty sure I was in the hotel illegally.

I awoke to find daylight blaring through the flimsy curtain. I lay there waiting to see whether the sun would hit the window. It did. It touched the poplar trees outside and turned their green leaves golden, then the welcome rays slid over the glass and into the room. Behind the trees was a bright blue sky.

The sight of the sun made me feel brave enough to get out of bed and face the cold. The female room attendant – smiling! – brought me hot water for washing and tea.

The main street of Dhongsheng was dominated by an imposing mosque that stood at one end of the street and looked down into the town. There are twenty thousand Muslims in Inner Mongolia. I noticed a crowd of people coming and going to and from a building in the main street. Remembering BB's advice, I deduced that it might be a shop. It was in fact a big market: a two-storeyed hall of stalls selling all manner of things. I bought a Chinese-English dictionary for eight *yuan*. The bus station was near by. It was also a market, with stalls selling food and bits and pieces for travel, like purses. I bought one. I was a bit short on purses after the day before. There was not a great deal of buying going on, but a surfeit of assistants lolled about. One slept soundly on the counter, another knitted.

A helpful man guessed what I was looking for and directed me to the loo. Again it cost two *fan* and was a public exhibition job. Inside I was confronted by two more doorways. I couldn't read the signs so I took pot luck and hoped I had chosen the ladies. This time I did not have an audience, which was just as well as I had to take off my coat and hang it over the door frame. I had heard people lose things this way if there's no one around to stop a thief, but it was quite impossible to use a squat toilet wearing the equivalent of a two-man tent. I had learned that the local word for toilet was pronounced 'cesspit' – how terribly right they were.

I asked a girl at one of the stalls where I could buy a ticket to Yinjinhuoluo, the village nearest the tomb of Ghenghis Khan, by showing her the Chinese for it in my book. The woman behind the ticket counter regarded me with distaste as I attempted to say Yinjinhuoluo. Then her attention was distracted by a workmate's knitting that had to be inspected. This took some time and a lot of conversation. I was ignored, as was fitting to a foreigner who did not speak a civilised tongue, until they had finished their business. Then the woman returned to ignoring me. I persisted, repeating my efforts to pronounce the word. I tried to show her the book, but she turned away disdainfully. I stayed stuck to the counter until, still refusing to look at me, she threw a ticket in my direction.

20 The last bus!

My bus did not leave for another hour so I sat down to wait. A beggar approached me timidly. There were three or four of them in the bus station and they looked utterly destitute. One old woman walked with difficulty, leaning on a stick and dragging her worldly goods and household effects behind her in a tattered hessian bag. I wanted to cry.

I bought a red sausage and a dry slab of sponge cake from the limited selection of food available, a wonderfully balanced and nutritional meal. The locals flocked and stood in a semi-circle to watch the amazing spectacle of the foreigner eating. Among them were several small children with split knickers. I wondered if their little posteriors were cold.

Soon I progressed to sitting in the warmth of the sun in a dilapidated bus in the station yard. I had a ticket but once again couldn't be sure where I was going. I hoped it was to the Great Khan's Mausoleum, but I wouldn't care if it wasn't. The journey's the thing, as Mark Twain said.

Suddenly we were off. Our driver started slowly, picking up extra people as he made his way out of the big yard.

Then another rival bus loomed up behind him and all hell broke loose. The conductor shouted and yelled, and the driver threw the bus into gear and roared off, blocking the other bus. He swerved past another smaller bus, scraping off some paint as he did so. Beating the rival bus to the exit, he squeezed through the traffic jam with only one minor collision; he swiped the rear-view mirror off another vehicle. No one took any notice and we continued on.

Our bus had two conductors. One sold tickets and smoked, the other was the shouter. He hung precariously out of the ancient door – which was held up by string and had cracked glass roughly mended with sticky tape – and roared our destination to the people on the streets. He was also the grabber, shover and stuffer; he squeezed people and their belongings into the bus.

We were held up at a road repair site where council workers, using shovels, were laying asphalt from an old boiler. Two of them, a man and a girl, shovelled and worked, while six others stood around them in an admiring circle, leaning on their implements. It must be international practice.

Most of the male passengers climbed aboard the bus smoking, and smoked the entire time they were on it. People only stopped smoking in order to chew sunflower seeds or spit. This disproved the crank health food theory that eating sunflower seeds stops the urge for nicotine. Most of the serious spitting was done out of the windows, but the men spat the seed husks on the floor. Sunflower seeds were also consumed with gusto by the conductors and the driver. The latter gentleman wore cotton gloves that were meant to be white. For an unfathomable reason, drivers of any vehicle, even old carts, wore these white cotton gloves. Our conductors climbed about the bus with a big green beer bottle in one hand and a cigarette in the other.

Anything unwanted was flung on the floor of the bus or out of the window. An empty beer bottle was thrown onto a concrete path in front of a workshop where vehicles were going in and out. It smashed to smithereens, scattering glass widely. No one batted an eyelash.

After two and a half hours I saw a colourful domed building standing alone on a hilltop surrounded by wilderness. 'Yinjinhuolou?' I asked the conductor. He nodded vigorously and I scrabbled over the obstacles to get out.

The bus roared off. I looked around and saw nothing except a handful of mud brick village houses lining a wide, dusty road. Willow and poplar trees flowed in groves down the hill slopes to the pasture land that stretched below. The country, and particularly the quietness, reminded me of Australia. I realised that it had been a long time since I had been anywhere this tranquil.

I set off down the hill in the direction of the mausoleum, which I could see about two kilometres away. Turning off onto a small track, I continued through waving grasslands where sheep and cows grazed. Eventually I arrived at a gate, where I looked up to see flight after flight of wide paved steps that led up to the imposing tomb on top of the hill.

The mausoleum was built in 1954 to honour the Great Khan and is supposed to house his ashes. Although Mongolians believe that he is buried somewhere in the Khenty Mountains and the location of his tomb remains a secret, the mausoleum is still regarded as a site of pilgrimage. Since the recent increase in Mongolian nationalistic fervour, Ghenghis Khan had been elevated to almost God-like status. It had become a sacred duty for all Mongolians to come to the mausoleum to pay homage to their hero. Ceremonies to honour him were held four times a year. Whole cooked sheep and burning butter lamps were placed before his large stone statue, and *khadags*, the blue ritual scarves, were presented while Mongolian monks chanted blessings.

It was late in the season and I had the place almost to myself. The walls were painted with bright murals depicting the exploits of the Khan – mainly battles and joyous conquering-hero-coming-home scenes.

The building also contained three elaborately decorated *gers*, which were replicas of the *gers* in which the Khan and his relatives had lived. These were surrounded by their martial and horse gear. The Khan's large *ger* was covered with the skins of snow leopards – no wonder they are rare and endangered. Inside, resting on his bier, was the shrine that supposedly contained the Khan's ashes.

Eventually I wandered back towards the road and, just as I came in sight of it, a bus rattled past. I walked up to the huddle of houses that constituted the village. They were small, with only two rooms, but all had chimneys; some had several. One building had a window in its front wall and looked a bit like a shop. It was open but empty. The place next door had three tables and a few chairs and seemed to be a cafe. I could see life in there, so I went in and asked the woman presiding over the establishment if I could sit down and wait for the bus. She smiled assent and kindly offered me tea, indicating that I should help myself from the big, battered thermos on the table. I offered to pay, but she shook her head. A man came in and in sign language told me that the buses came past every hour.

I took a drink of tea. It was heavily salted! Yuk. When the woman left the room, I tipped it back into the thermos. She returned, saw my empty glass and, beaming at me, refilled it. If you consider that warm water and salt is the original emetic, it will not be hard to imagine how that tea made me feel.

I sat by the window in a pool of sun. A large, comely, grey sow meandered past unattended. My pet pig, Mindy, much as she loved her home, would had been over the hills and far away if left to her own devices like that. A white nanny goat trotted past investigating the sides of the road – there were no footpaths – for possible edibles. Two small pigs squealed past with that mincing, ballet dancers' walk that little pigs execute when they are in a hurry. I also watched as a diminutive donkey picked her way down the hill, dragging a huge load of greenery behind her on an old wooden cart. She returned later with a small bale of hay and, finally, she came past, led on a rope and minus the cart, going home. I envied her. It was two hours later, the sun was setting, and I was still there.

This was a Mongolian village and the people spoke Mongolian. The woman shopkeeper had the obligatory one child – a handsome sturdy boy of about three. She also ran the shop next door, leaving the door open and trotting in there when a customer called to her.

An old man pedalled his bicycle utility to the shop to deliver a big load of sheepskins. Soon afterwards a three-wheeler motor bike with a cart on the back chugged to a stop outside the shop. It was loaded with the biggest cabbages I have ever seen. The woman went out to inspect them.

The cafe gradually filled with men who drank endless cups of tea and bottles of beer. They smoked ceaselessly until the cigarette fog in the small room was so bad I could hardly see.

As darkness fell I had to accept the fact that the bus I had missed had been the last one of the day. Several big trucks passed, but no cars, or I might have thumbed a ride. The men in the cafe told me that a car would be okay but warned me emphatically against the trucks.

They said the trucks would be too slow, but I felt there was something else they didn't say, so I took their advice. The trucks broke down constantly and I had heard that there was much smuggling and illegal activity, possibly even rebellion, in these parts.

I reflected on my situation. I was at Yinjinhuoluo, two-and-a-half bone-shaking hours by local bus from Dhongsheng, which was four hours by the same from Baotou, which was three hours from Hohot, which was thirteen and a bit hours by soft sleeper from Beijing. It was the dark of night and I was homeless, without a toothbrush or a change of undies. I thanked heaven that I had paid two nights in advance for my room back in Dhongseng, or my baggage might have been out on the street by now.

I realised that I would have to stay the night. My hostess was unperturbed and indicated that I could sleep there.

For dinner I gnawed my way along several large sheep shanks. These had been thrown onto a gigantic plate accompanied by a murderous butcher's knife for use as an eating implement. I asked for a bottle of beer – anything to prevent a reappearance of the lethal tea. An old tin basin roosted in an iron stand in a corner of the room for the purpose of hand washing. The village had no running water. Earlier I had seen a man jog by bearing two buckets on a yoke on his shoulders. He was the local water supply.

My hostess showed me the small front room where I could sleep. I got out my book and pointed to what I thought was 'toilet', but I was actually pointing cross-eyed to 'hotel'. The woman indicated the room. I couldn't see where she meant me to go. Eventually my message got through to her. She answered volubly, but I failed to understand. She raised her eyebrows and grinned widely as if to say, God help me, these foreigners can't even find their way to the toilet when everyone knows you go in the street. She took my hand, pushed me out the door, whacking me jovially on the bottom as I went, and frog-marched me across the road to the communal village loo. The gates were locked. We went further up the road to another loo. Its gates were also locked. Having exhausted all possibilities, she took me around a corner, dropped her pants and squatted. So did I.

As I stood in the road, I could see the mausoleum in the distance. Ethereal and dreamy, alone on its hill top, it was brightly lit by a full moon. I would never have guessed when I set out to find the Great Khan's shrine that I would end up seeing it by moonlight.

My room for the night was tiny and had only enough space for the three narrow single beds that were crammed in side by side, almost touching. The walls of plastered mud-brick were dirty and scarred. A bare light bulb hung from the ceiling on a cord, and an old metal washstand held a tin washbasin. The door, which opened directly onto the road out the front, looked home made. It needed a hefty kick to shut it and a good pull to open it. There was no lock.

The landlady brought me a bowl of hot water so that I could wash. It was a pity I had nothing to wash with. I only had the clothes I had on and my handbag. I would sleep in my bottom two layers of clothes; all other niceties I would have to do without. It was reasonably warm in the room as it backed onto the kitchen where there was a fire for cooking. It had become bitterly cold outside the moment the sun had disappeared.

The beds were made from lumps of unfinished wood, splintered and banged together casually. Nails protruded. The base was made from several planks with hessian nailed over them, and a flattened cardboard carton covered by one thin cotton quilt served as a mattress. Good for the back, but murder for my poor aging hips. The usual small square pillow and a satin-cased quilt completed the sleeping outfit.

But beggars cannot be choosers. I slept well, and I was warm and cosy, despite the noise. Ancient trucks lumbered past now and then, making a terrible row as they groaned to the top of the hill. It was a Saturday night, and my refuge was apparently the equivalent of a downtown disco. The last rowdy patron left at eleven, a wild late night by local standards.

Next day being Sunday, I fervently hoped that the buses didn't take the day off. But I was told that the first bus came through at seven, or at nine. Suit yourself! I installed myself in my position in the front window, wondering if this was some kind of world record; more than sixteen hours waiting for a bus. Water ran down the windows as the frost melted in the sun. Half-past seven came and went and there was no bus. The grey sow sauntered past in the opposite direction from yesterday. The donkey also returned, starting work early for a Sunday. Men began to come out of doors and spit. One headed off across the road with a tin basin and when he returned I could see steam rising from it. I presumed he went to get hot water to wash or shave. A shower would be out of the question here. Two other hopeful travellers deposited bags by the road and appeared to be waiting for the bus. They were Mongolian, so I trusted that they knew more than I did. The cafe was soon filled with half a dozen men noisily siphoning up tea. It seemed to be the men's club. Men did everything together here – trooping across the road, eating at the cafe – but I saw no women apart from my landlady.

I felt I now knew everyone and their animals in this village by sight. The landlady offered me breakfast: a big steaming bowl of thick noodles in a tasty soup thick with bits and pieces probably left over from the night before. Not scrapings off the plates, I hoped. I slurped it up.

Suddenly, at half-past eight, not seven or nine as promised, there was the bus! The most wonderful sight in the world. I thanked my hostess profusely, paid her the ten *yuan* she asked for my board and lodging, and rushed out. I climbed aboard and found a seat. The passengers were mostly male, and they were blatantly fascinated with me. The conductor addressed me as *Loala* (foreigner), but in a pleasant way. He sold me a ticket for six *yuan*, cheaper by three *yuan* than the outward journey, and I was on my way.

We broke down once on the top of an extremely steep hill. A couple of trucks came by and drove around us, probably well used to the sight of a broken down bus. The driver took the engine cover off and fiddled about for a bit, then tried to jump start the bus by rolling it backwards down the hill. This was certainly not one of the best feelings I have ever had – careering downhill in reverse in a bus with who knows what sort of brakes, on the edge of a precipice. Finally the bus coughed into life and we set off again.

An old man, waiting by the side of the lonely country road, hailed the bus. He was surrounded by ten large assorted bundles that included four wheat bags full of spuds. There was a furious argument between the old man, the driver and the conductors. I think they were saying that his luggage was excessive. By now the bus was crammed full. We had been picking up people and their cargo along the way, and the aisles were choc-a-block with bundles and bags. The argument ended with smiles and jokes, and everyone helped load the old man and his bundles aboard.

The return journey to Dhongseng was shorter than the outward one as we went as fast as the gas pedal would allow. The old bus jolted and banged along the road. If those slimming machines work, where you are put in a harness and shaken about madly, then I must have lost several kilos on this ride.

My elderly neighbour smoked evil local cigars non-stop until his head began to droop. Lower and lower it sank, until finally it rested on my chest just below my shoulder. With all his weight leaning against me, he began to snore, causing his hair to go up and down and brush my chin rhythmically. I stared down into his dusty black hair and hoped it wasn't the home of any livestock.

A girl got on the bus wearing her Sunday best, ready for the bright lights and gay times of downtown Dhongseng. She was dressed in gold platform shoes with straps, buckles and four-inch Louis heels, maroon and black patterned socks, brown, yellow and apricot striped flared pants, and a red jumper under a lime green and yellow, checked jacket. A big gold hair ornament crowned the lot. She looked like she had got dressed out of the Salvos cast-off bin. It was my turn to stare, thinking that if this was the outfit for a Sunday morning, what would a big night out bring on?

Safely back at the hotel in Dhongseng once more, I received quite a reaction from the girl in attendance. I was not sure if she was shocked, or pleased, to see me. She called out to the manager, '*Loala*' and something, possibly, 'The foreigner's back.' I tried to explain. I showed them the mausoleum admission ticket and they understood at last that I'd been away. Maybe they thought I'd been out on the town; it had been Saturday night. They probably had grave doubts about the morals of all foreigners, who are generally believed to be licentious and depraved.

By the time I'd had a badly needed wash, a cup of tea and some noodles, I was restored enough to go out and walk on the Sunday streets. This was enjoyable. Everyone was out strolling, visiting, shopping, gossiping or doing their washing, which they hung anywhere they could – in the street on wooden stands or swinging across the footpaths on ropes. The pavements were sprinkled with people selling goods hung on makeshift stands or on strings from trees. Thinking they were just what I needed, I tried to buy some longjohns that were hanging on a tree in front of a shop. I was finally convinced that they were not for sale – it was someone's washing!

There were also birds for sale, mostly pigeons that I feared were for eating. Repair men set themselves up among the passers-by with a few tools of trade. Among them were many bicycle fixers who were identified by the bowl of water they used for testing bike tubes. Apart from the big indoor market and the bus station stalls, the only other shops were tiny, hole in the wall affairs. There was, however, a large pharmacy. The two female staff were busy with their knitting. The large room had glass-topped wooden counters all the way around it, housing multitudes of Chinese medicines. One long wall was entirely covered by antique wooden drawers about eight inches square. These had wooden knobs and the names of their contents written across them in wonderful red Chinese characters.

Fortune tellers were out on the streets in droves to catch the Sunday strollers. They sat cross-legged on the footpath with their red horoscope charts spread out in front of them. When they lured a customer, they dealt little cards or pieces of paper around the chart and made predictions such as, 'You will go on a long journey over much water and meet a tall, dark, handsome stranger.' I saved my money. I did not need to be told this. I've been there. Done that. But I'm still waiting for the last bit.

Passing the bus station I was accosted by a smiling girl selling tickets outside. 'Baotou?' she said. Hooray! I finally understood a Chinese word. I got out my book to point to the word for 'tomorrow'. She in turn pointed to ten on the clock.

Back in my room in the late afternoon, I sat in the armchair and watched the goings on in the street. As soon as the sun disappeared, the cold began to seep through the window. Even with my down coat over my knees, I was soon thoroughly chilled. To escape the cold, I went across the street to an unpretentious place that served food. For eighty-five cents I had a large bottle of beer and as much as I could possibly eat, with sauces and a dish of pickled cabbage thrown in for nothing. I was only ever charged local prices in Inner Mongolia, except for the first hotel. This made a refreshing change.

Getting my meal was a hilarious experience. I had the entire staff – the cook, the waiter and the manager – as well as the one other customer, poring over my book trying to find something for me to eat. At one stage, when the ticket for Ghenghis Khan's mausoleum fell out of my book, it was pounced on and wondered over. My new friends were terribly impressed that I had gone all the way to Yinjinhuoluo to pay homage to the Great Khan.

The friendly customer offered me a large glassful of the appalling Chinese whisky I had already tasted. I declined, charmingly, I hoped. Shortly afterwards, he came over to me and tried to put a cigarette in my hand. I drew the line at that. I might try Chinese whisky, but I'd sooner have a live snake in my hand than a cigarette. The customer obviously thought he knew what foreign women liked. I pondered what his next offer would be.

I am ashamed to admit that by half-past seven I was in

bed. Worse. I have to confess that I had actually wanted to go to bed at four, as it was the only place I could get warm. The long awaited fifteenth of October had come and gone, but the government had not turned on the heat as promised. I bore them a terrible grudge.

I was fed and I was warm. Sitting in bed with a good book, I wallowed in luxury. There are moments when you are travelling when you are supremely happy, and these are usually brief. They occur when you experience the sort of comfort you take for granted at home. I think the attraction and challenge of travel are about overcoming the traumas, obstacles and difficulties that prevent you from attaining this state. You feel terrific when you make it safely to your destination and are rested and restored. Much as I preferred Mongolia to China, for example, I had to leave because of the cold. I decided to travel back to Beijing and head south from there.

In the interests of hygiene, I braved the freezing morning cold to wash my hair in the basin, using a thermos of hot water. On the stairs outside the hotel a good-hearted passer-by stopped to help me flag down a pedal cart and negotiate a fare to the bus station.

At the bus station, the ticket-touting girl from the day before greeted me warmly and directed me to a bus. All was well, I thought. It was a big bus. The driver, however, seemed unaware of this. He took off in great haste and drove as though he were in a red MG sports.

I returned to Baotou bus terminal, the scene of my recent robbery. Wise in hindsight, I refused all help and got to the train station under my own steam. I wandered around like a lost sheep until a young woman, who was working in some sort of official capacity, adopted me. I realised that the offices were all shut for the usual two-hour lunch. My escort, unbeknown to me, had decided that I needed a hotel to sleep in until the train left at nine that night. Thinking that we were going somewhere to get a ticket, I followed my guide out of the station and through a winding maze of tiny crooked alleys. We went into a diminutive mud-brick hovel. I agreed to a single, yes, for one, yes, with bed, yes please. The penny dropped when I was escorted into a dark, dismal room. Even after I said, 'No thanks', they persisted. I made it clear that all I wanted was a train ticket, and we trudged back to the station, my friend a little disappointed. Still, we parted on good terms.

The ticket staff returned in a leisurely way from lunch. I stood in front of the counter while a woman with a very surly expression studiously ignored the waiting customers and prepared herself for business, performing her post-lunch rituals as though they were holy rites. She set out her money and unlocked everything. Even the tickets that hung on nails on a board had a wooden concertina rack that rolled over them to be locked. I had plenty of time to wonder how they thought someone could steal them while the Gorgon was at lunch when the room was also locked. When all was completed and the woman was unable to delay parting with her precious tickets any longer, she sat down resignedly.

I procured a ticket for a soft sleeper to Beijing. In the meantime, I had seven hours to while away. The first-class waiting room – I mean International Waiting Room – was locked against marauders, and would not be opened until one hour before the train arrived. I installed myself in the general purpose waiting room, a massive catacomb of a place with a ceiling sixty feet away from the terrazzo floor and double-glazed casement windows that reached from the ground to the roof. I took a seat near the entrance as far away as possible from the toilets, but I could still smell them.

I attracted a mob at once and in no time was faced

by a staring squad. They sat around me as closely as possible and peered open-mouthed and agog into my face. I took refuge behind my book. They took it from me to examine it. I got it back and they leaned over me from the side to continue looking at it, or stood in front of me to look at it upside down. It must have been a riveting read for them: *Travels With A Donkey* by R.L. Stevenson, in English, no pictures. Open a book anywhere in China, and it is a sure bet that someone will come and look at it. People will also pick up your postcards as you write them and try to read them. No one seemed to have any sense of individual property or privacy. My personal space was constantly invaded, even though people were usually only trying to be nice. Mostly this did not bother me.

To keep some of the audience at bay I moved to an end seat, but they lined up in front of it, three deep. A fearsome female guard, who looked like a bulldog, but far more ferocious, kept chasing my retinue away. This short, corpulent dragon patrolled the huge waiting room, like a prison guard or warder, only worse, shouting and screaming abuse at wrong-doers. One of the spectators was a small urchin who became my shadow for several hours. I attracted his attention outside and he, being young and impressionable, appeared to think that a close study of me would improve his education. He stayed stuck by my side absorbing everything I did until repeated assaults by the dragon lady finally cleared him off. He was about ten years old and dressed in tattered, filthy clothes. He gazed at me enraptured from the one of the dirtiest faces I have seen.

By four o'clock in the afternoon it was extremely cold in the waiting room. What a morgue! It must have been freezing in winter. Perhaps the heating helped when, and if, it was ever turned on. Exactly one hour before the train was due, I was collected by a uniformed young woman and ushered to the first-class waiting room, where the door was ceremoniously unlocked for me by the dragon. What luxury I entered. Once I was installed, the door was re-locked. Too bad if I needed to get out. The guard was incarcerated with me, her sole function being to watch me until nine o'clock when the train arrived.

This waiting room was, like everything in China, colossal. Ceilings up to the gods, floor-length windows, and a private door onto the station in front of which the first-class compartments of the train would be stopped. The floor was covered by a beautiful, thick blue Chinese carpet. There were plush red velvet armchairs with white lace anti-macassars and glass coffee tables. Everything looked spotlessly clean and unused.

The doors and windows had lace curtains and reflector film on the glass to keep those inside from the sight of the rabble. Occasionally one of the latter, a brave or foolish soul, rattled the doors and tried to breach the hallowed portals, but they were sent packing by the guard. So this was how the privileged few lived! It seemed unfair, but I imagined that if the riffraff were let in, it would have been wrecked in ten minutes flat. And I was grateful to escape the staring squad.

The train pulled in on time and the guard helped me to my comfortable compartment. I was initially the only occupant, but later I was joined by two gents. During the night we passed the remote place from where I could have set out to find the remains of Khubla Khan's 'stately pleasure dome'. Xanadu would have to stay mysterious and elusive and, like Coleridge's poem, only something to remember. Lost in the loneliness of the open grasslands, only a tumbled heap of stones and a few acres of broken earth wall remain of the once fabulous city and marvellous palace. These had been taken apart stone by stone to be used for local huts or walls. But this was a restricted area, and I had not been able to get a permit to enter.

A cold grey day dawned. I had breakfast in the dining car. I was served large slabs of dry white bread, a glass of hot milk and jam and sugar cubes in pottery dishes. This was what the cook imagined to be a suitable breakfast for a foreigner. I rejected it politely and pointed to the food the Chinese had: thick noodles in broth topped by two flat, oily fried eggs. I could now eat a fried egg with chopsticks quite easily, if not elegantly.

From Badaling I saw once again the mighty Wall. The weather was becoming slightly warmer. At the Beijing station I achieved the marathon task of finding the ticket office. The next train to Tianjin on the coast left at seven that night. Even though this meant another wait of four hours, I bought a ticket on it. I didn't want to spend the night in Beijing. Once again a grumpy woman threw the ticket at me, but I was used to being treated like a foreigner. I didn't care any more. I was heading south and I had heard that the southern Chinese were much nicer to 'big noses'. I planned to reach Tianjin, take a ship from there to Shanghai and then go down the Yangtze by river boat. Continuing to head south, I hoped to make it to the border of North Vietnam. From there, visa permitting, I would go down through that country to Ho Chi Min City, get on a plane, and be home for Christmas. My spirits revived at the thought of southern warmth and, stepping on the train, I headed home.

Also by Lydia Laube

Wakefield Press is an independent publishing and
distribution company based in Adelaide, South Australia.
We love good stories and publish beautiful books.
To see our full range of books, please visit our website at
www.wakefieldpress.com.au
where all titles are available for purchase.
To keep up with our latest releases, news and events,
subscribe to our monthly newsletter.

Find us!

Facebook: www.facebook.com/wakefield.press
Twitter: www.twitter.com/wakefieldpress
Instagram: www.instagram.com/wakefieldpress

www.ingramcontent.com/pod-product-compliance
Lightning Source LLC
Chambersburg PA
CBHW031831090426
42741CB00005B/201